JANE
ADDAMS

AMERICAN WOMEN of ACHIEVEMENT

JANE ADDAMS

MARY KITTREDGE

CHELSEA HOUSE PUBLISHERS

NEW YORK • PHILADELPHIA

EDITOR-IN-CHIEF: Nancy Toff
EXECUTIVE EDITOR: Remmel T. Nunn
MANAGING EDITOR: Karyn Gullen Browne
COPY CHIEF: Juliann Barbato
PICTURE EDITOR: Adrian G. Allen
ART DIRECTOR: Giannella Garrett
MANUFACTURING MANAGER: Gerald Levine

Staff for JANE ADDAMS

SENIOR EDITOR: Constance Jones
TEXT EDITOR: Marian W. Taylor
COPYEDITOR: James Guiry
DEPUTY COPY CHIEF: Ellen Scordato
EDITORIAL ASSISTANT: Theodore Keyes
PICTURE RESEARCHER: Justine Blau
DESIGNER: Design Oasis
DESIGN ASSISTANT: Donna Sinisgalli
PRODUCTION COORDINATOR: Joseph Romano
COVER ILLUSTRATOR: Donna Perrone

3   5   7   9   8   6   4

Library of Congress Cataloging in Publication Data

Kittredge, Mary, 1949–
Jane Addams.

(American women of achievement)
Bibliography: p.
   Includes index.
1. Addams, Jane, 1860–1935—Juvenile literature.
2. Social workers—United States—Biography—Juvenile literature.
I. Title. II. Series. HV28.A35K4   1988   361′.92′4   [B]   87-27662
ISBN 1-55546-636-2
   0-7910-0406-6 (pbk.)

CONTENTS

AMERICAN WOMEN of ACHIEVEMENT

Abigail Adams
women's rights advocate

Jane Addams
social worker

Louisa May Alcott
author

Marian Anderson
singer

Susan B. Anthony
woman suffragist

Ethel Barrymore
actress

Clara Barton
founder of the American Red Cross

Elizabeth Blackwell
physician

Nellie Bly
journalist

Margaret Bourke-White
photographer

Pearl Buck
author

Rachel Carson
biologist and author

Mary Cassatt
artist

Agnes De Mille
choreographer

Emily Dickinson
poet

Isadora Duncan
dancer

Amelia Earhart
aviator

Mary Baker Eddy
founder of the Christian Science church

Betty Friedan
feminist

Althea Gibson
tennis champion

Emma Goldman
political activist

Helen Hayes
actress

Lillian Hellman
playwright

Katharine Hepburn
actress

Karen Horney
psychoanalyst

Anne Hutchinson
religious leader

Mahalia Jackson
gospel singer

Helen Keller
humanitarian

Jeane Kirkpatrick
diplomat

Emma Lazarus
poet

Clare Boothe Luce
author and diplomat

Barbara McClintock
biologist

Margaret Mead
anthropologist

Edna St. Vincent Millay
poet

Julia Morgan
architect

Grandma Moses
painter

Louise Nevelson
sculptor

Sandra Day O'Connor
Supreme Court justice

Georgia O'Keeffe
painter

Eleanor Roosevelt
diplomat and humanitarian

Wilma Rudolph
champion athlete

Florence Sabin
medical researcher

Beverly Sills
opera singer

Gertrude Stein
author

Gloria Steinem
feminist

Harriet Beecher Stowe
author and abolitionist

Mae West
entertainer

Edith Wharton
author

Phillis Wheatley
poet

Babe Didrikson Zaharias
champion athlete

CHELSEA HOUSE PUBLISHERS

"Remember the Ladies"

MATINA S. HORNER

Remember the Ladies." That is what Abigail Adams wrote to her husband John, then a delegate to the Continental Congress, as the Founding Fathers met in Philadelphia to form a new nation in March of 1776. "Be more generous and favorable to them than your ancestors. Do not put such unlimited power in the hands of the Husbands. If particular care and attention is not paid to the Ladies," Abigail Adams warned, "we are determined to foment a Rebellion, and will not hold ourselves bound by any Laws in which we have no voice, or Representation."

The words of Abigail Adams, one of the earliest American advocates of women's rights, were prophetic. Because when we have not "remembered the ladies," they have, by their words and deeds, reminded us so forcefully of the omission that we cannot fail to remember them. For the history of American women is as interesting and varied as the history of our nation as a whole. American women have played an integral part in founding, settling, and building our country. Some we remember as remarkable women who—against great odds—achieved distinction in the public arena: Anne Hutchinson, who in the 17th century became a charismatic religious leader; Phillis Wheatley, an 18th-century black slave who became a poet; Susan B. Anthony, whose name is synonymous with the 19th-century women's rights movement, and who led the struggle to enfranchise women; and, in our own century, Amelia Earhart, the first woman to cross the Atlantic Ocean by air.

These extraordinary women certainly merit our admiration, but other women, "common women," many of them all but forgotten, should also be recognized for their contributions to American thought and culture. Women have been community builders; they have founded schools and formed voluntary associations to help those in need; they have assumed the major responsibility for rearing children, passing on from one generation to the next the values that keep a culture alive. These and innumerable other contributions, once ignored, are now being recognized by scholars, students, and the public. It is exciting and gratifying to realize that a part of our history that was hardly acknowledged a few generations ago is now being studied and brought to light.

In recent decades, the field of women's history has grown from obscurity to a politically controversial splinter movement to academic respectability, in many cases mainstreamed into such traditional disciplines as history, economics, and psychology. Scholars of women, both female and male, have organized research centers at such prestigious institutions as Wellesley College, Stanford University, and the University of California. Other notable centers for women's studies are the Center for the American Woman and Politics at the Eagleton Institute of Politics at Rutgers University; the Henry A. Murray Research Center for the Study of Lives, at Radcliffe College; and the Women's Research and Education Institute, the research arm of the Congressional Caucus on Women's Issues. Other scholars and public figures have established archives and libraries, such as the Schlesinger Library on the History of Women in America, at Radcliffe College, and the Sophia Smith Collection, at Smith College, to collect and preserve the written and tangible legacies of women.

From the initial donation of the Women's Rights Collection in 1943, the Schlesinger Library grew to encompass vast collections documenting the manifold accomplishments of American women. Simultaneously, the women's movement in general and the academic discipline of women's studies in particular also began with a narrow definition and gradually expanded their mandate. Early causes such as woman suffrage and social reform, abolition and organized labor were joined by newer concerns such as the history of women in business and the professions and in politics and government; the study of the family; and social issues such as health policy and education.

Women, as historian Arthur M. Schlesinger, jr., once pointed out, "have constituted the most spectacular casualty of traditional history. They have made up at least half the human race, but you could never tell that by looking at the books historians write." The new breed of historians is remedying that omission. They have written books about immigrant women and about working-class women who struggled for survival in cities and about black women who met the challenges of life in rural areas. They are telling the stories of women who, despite the barriers of tradition and economics, became lawyers and doctors and public figures.

The women's studies movement has also led scholars to question traditional interpretations of their respective disciplines. For example, the study of war has traditionally been an exercise in military and political analysis, an examination of strategies planned and executed by men. But scholars of women's history have pointed out that wars have also been periods of tremendous change and even opportunity for women, because the very absence of men on the home front enabled them to expand their educational, economic, and professional activities and to assume leadership in their homes.

The early scholars of women's history showed a unique brand of courage in choosing to investigate new subjects and take new approaches to old ones. Often, like their subjects, they endured criticism and even ostracism by their academic colleagues. But their efforts have unquestionably been worthwhile, because with the publication of each new study and book another piece of the historical patchwork is sewn into place, revealing an increasingly comprehensive picture of the role of women in our rich and varied history.

Such books on groups of women are essential, but books that focus on the lives of individuals are equally indispensable. Biographies can be inspirational, offering their readers the example of people with vision who have looked outside themselves for their goals and have often struggled against great obstacles to achieve them. Marian Anderson, for instance, had to overcome racial bigotry in order to perfect her art and perform as a concert singer. Isadora Duncan defied the rules of classical dance to find true artistic freedom. Jane Addams had to break down society's notions of the proper role for women in order to create new social institutions, notably the settlement house. All of these women had to come to terms both with themselves and with the world in which they lived. Only then could they move ahead as pioneers in their chosen callings.

Biography can inspire not only by adulation but also by realism. It helps us to see not only the qualities in others that we hope to emulate, but also, perhaps, the weaknesses that made them "human." By helping us identify with the subject on a more personal level they help us to feel that we, too, can achieve such goals. We read about Eleanor Roosevelt, for instance, who occupied a unique and seemingly enviable position as the wife of the president. Yet we can sympathize with her inner dilemma: an inherently shy woman, she had to force herself to live a most public life in order to use her position to benefit others. We may not be able to imagine ourselves having the immense poetic talent of Emily Dickinson, but from her story we can understand the challenges faced by a creative woman who was expected to fulfill many family responsibilities. And though few of us will ever reach the level of athletic accomplishment displayed by Wilma Rudolph or Babe Zaharias, we can still appreciate their spirit, their overwhelming will to excel.

A biography is a multifaceted lens. It is first of all a magnification, the intimate examination of one particular life. But at the same time, it is a wide-angle lens, informing us about the world in which the subject lived. We come away from reading about one life knowing more about the social, political, and economic fabric of the time. It is for this reason, perhaps, that the great New England essayist Ralph Waldo Emerson wrote, in 1841, "There is properly no history: only biography." And it is also why biography, and particularly women's biography, will continue to fascinate writers and readers alike.

JANE
ADDAMS

At 28, Jane Addams had not yet decided what to do with her life. She was, she said, "absolutely at sea so far as any moral purpose was concerned."

ONE

"Living Next Door to Poverty"

It was a sunny afternoon in April 1888. At the Plaza de Toros in Madrid, Spain, the bullfight was about to begin. A holiday atmosphere prevailed as the cheerful, noisy crowd surged into the arena, eager to watch the dangerous contest between man and animal. The air seemed to crackle with excitement. Not everyone in the arena, however, shared the mood of high-spirited anticipation.

Among the spectators were five American women who were touring Europe. Four of them regarded the scene with grim faces, clearly apprehensive about the blood that would soon be shed. The fifth, 28-year-old Jane Addams of Cedarville, Illinois, was different. Wide-eyed and smiling, she was unmistakably elated by the color, the music, the pageantry of the

bullring. "The riders on the caparisoned horses," she later wrote, "might have been knights of a tournament, or the matador a slightly armed gladiator facing his martyrdom."

Driven to a frenzy by the sharp wooden lances of the *picadores*, the first bull galloped toward its tormentors, tossing several of their horses with its wickedly curved horns. The crowd roared, and Addams found herself on her feet, cheering as loudly as the rest. Her friends hurriedly left the arena, but she stayed until five bulls had been killed.

Later, writing to a friend about the spectacle, she called it the "great event" of her stay in Madrid. It was, she said, "the most brilliant affair . . . I have ever seen. The excitement and interest were so great as to throw the

13

A matador confronts his opponent in Madrid. Bullfighting thrilled Jane Addams at first, but she later referred to the sport as "a wrong thing."

cruelty and brutality quite into the background."

When Addams's friends asked her how she could have enjoyed watching animals suffer, she responded defensively at first. The contest, she pointed out, formed part of the culture they had all come to Europe to absorb. Surely, she said, there was no real harm in it. As the memory of the bullring's excitement receded, however, she started to reconsider her position.

The violent spectacle had been thrilling, true. The bullfighters had been graceful, brave, and skillful; the blaring trumpets, the riotously colored flowers, the shouting crowds, had been almost hypnotically compelling. But the fight, Addams realized, had not been a fair one. Although the men risked their lives, they had chosen to compete. The animals had been given no choice.

"Greatly to my surprise and horror," Addams later wrote, "I found I had seen, with comparative indifference, five bulls and many more horses killed." The more she thought about it, the more she felt she had made a mistake. It was all too easy, she observed in a letter to another friend, to let color and excitement lead to the "concealing of a wrong thing."

Jane Addams had dreamed of serving humanity. "Long before the end of my school days," she recalled in her autobiography, "it was quite settled in my mind that I should study medicine and 'live with the poor.' " So far, however, she had done neither. At this point in her life, she scolded herself, she "was absolutely at sea so far as any moral purpose was concerned." Un-

Homeless Londoners sleep in a public park in the 1890s. Addams was appalled by the widespread poverty she saw during her 1888 visit to the British capital.

married, wealthy, and uncertain of exactly how she could "minister to human needs," she had put off thinking about the matter and come to Europe for culture and amusement.

The afternoon she spent at the Plaza de Toros had a profound influence on her life. Meditating about the experience, she decided that, far from doing anything good with her life, she was in danger of losing her ability to recognize evil. Applauding cruelty went against her deepest ideals, yet she had done it. She must not, she decided, go on wasting her time, letting her convictions fade. "I had fallen into the meanest type of self-deception," she wrote later, "in making myself believe that all this [study and travel] was in preparation for great things to come. Nothing less than the moral reaction following the ... bullfight had been

able to reveal to me that ... I had been tied to the tail of the oxcart of self-seeking."

The day after the bullfight, Addams had a long conversation with her good friend and traveling companion Ellen Starr. She told Starr about an idea she had been considering for some time. She envisioned establishing a residence for privileged young women among the poor, a place where they "might try out some of the things they had been taught," and "learn of life from life itself." Such a residence, Addams thought, might benefit both well-educated but inexperienced young women and the poor people among whom they would live. She was particularly concerned about the struggling newcomers to America, "those groups of homesick immigrants huddled together in strange tenement houses"

15

Arnold Toynbee, a British sociologist and economist, was also a pioneering social worker. Toynbee Hall, which opened in 1884, was named for him.

whom she had observed during earlier visits to Chicago.

Starr was enthusiastic about her friend's tentative plan. After days of conversation about it, Addams later recalled, "the scheme had become convincing and tangible, although still most hazy in detail." Addams had heard that in London several experimental residences similar to the one she had in mind had been established, and she decided to go and see them for herself. Cancelling the rest of her European tour, she headed for the British capital.

She was particularly interested in learning about two of the "wonderful places" she had heard about: Toynbee Hall and the People's Palace. These institutions, described by the new term *settlement houses*, aimed to bridge the huge gulf between Britain's upper and lower classes. Operating in the slums of London, they were staffed by cultured and well-to-do men and women who offered workshops, libraries, classes, and meeting rooms to their new neighbors.

The volunteers at Toynbee Hall and the People's Palace rejected the traditional "charity" approach to aiding the poor; instead of sending their servants with occasional baskets of food or coal, they literally moved in with the people they hoped to help. This concept appealed strongly to Jane Addams.

She was especially impressed by Toynbee Hall, which she described in a letter to a friend as "so free from 'professional doing good,' so unaffectedly sincere and so productive of good results in its classes and libraries so that it seems perfectly ideal." Here were people, she said admiringly, who were "perpetually disturbed over the apparent inequalities of mankind."

Inspired by what she saw in London, Addams began to form a clear plan of action. No longer would she simply yearn to "minister to human needs"; she would put her idealism into action. She would, she decided, go home and start a settlement house like Toynbee

Hall. Precisely what she would do there she was not yet certain, but she felt sure she would learn as she went along.

"Whatever perplexities and discouragement concerning the life of the poor were in store for me," she wrote later, "I should at least know something at first hand and have the solace of daily activity. I had confidence that . . . the period of mere passive receptivity had come to an end, and I had at last finished with the everlasting 'preparation for life,' however ill-prepared I might be."

Addams had never made decisions quickly, but when she made one, she stuck to it. Her father, a hardworking Pennsylvania Quaker who had made a modest fortune as an Illinois banker and real estate dealer, had taught her to have high ideals—and to live up to them. Jane Addams's firmness of purpose carried her through months of planning and preparation, and on September 18, 1889, she ceased her "everlasting preparation for life" and began to live it.

On that day, nearly a year and a half after the bullfight that had stirred her conscience, Addams climbed the front steps of Hull House, a rundown mansion in Chicago that she and Ellen Starr had rented. Built in 1856 by a wealthy real estate dealer, the house had been one of the few in the area to escape the Great Chicago Fire of 1871. In the years that followed the fire, the

Firefighters struggle to control the Great Chicago Fire of 1871. The blaze, the worst in the nation's history, killed 300 people and left 100,000 homeless.

once-prosperous neighborhood had become home to thousands of European immigrants who had fled their native countries hoping to find a better life in America.

Because few of these immigrants spoke English or understood American ways, they were able to get only the most menial, low-paying jobs. Whole families, including small children, labored for pennies a day in factories and slaughterhouses. Barely earning enough to survive, they sank deeper and deeper into poverty. By the time Addams arrived, the Hull House neighborhood had become one of Chicago's worst slums.

"Little idea can be given of the filthy and rotten tenements, the foul stables and dilapidated outhouses, the piles of garbage fairly alive with diseased odors, and the numbers of children filling every nook [and] seeming literally to pave every scrap of yard," wrote one contemporary witness about the neighborhood.

In her own description of the area,

Addams wrote: "The streets are inexpressibly dirty, the schools inadequate, sanitary legislation unenforced, the

Ruined homes and factories are all that remain after the Chicago fire. Hull House (above right) was spared by the flames, which destroyed 17,500 other buildings.

street lighting bad, the paving miserable.... Many houses have no water supply save the faucet in the backyard, [and] there are no fire escapes."

In this neighborhood, in fact, almost everything was wrong that could be wrong—which was exactly why Addams and Starr had chosen to live there. It was not enough merely to visit the poor. "We need," Addams wrote, "the thrust in the side that comes from living next door to poverty." On that September morning she unlocked the mansion's battered front door, opening not only Hull House but an important chapter in American social history.

Addams and Starr began to settle into their new home immediately. "Probably no young matron ever placed her own things in her own house with more pleasure than that with which we first furnished Hull House," Addams later said. The two women hung reproductions of oil paintings on the old walls, and Addams even set her heirloom silver tea service in the sideboard, despite friends' warnings that thieves would surely break in and steal it.

Addams did not share such grim expectations. She believed in concentrating on people's high potential, not their low circumstances—and she decided to begin as she meant to go on, with trust in her neighbors' basic decency. Her confidence proved well-founded almost at once. Excited by the

A neighborhood policeman looks on as a group of immigrant women and children gather outside Hull House in the early 1890s.

first day in their new home, the women forgot to lock, or even to close, the doors when they went to bed. The house stood open all that night, but in the morning nothing in it had been disturbed. "We were much pleased," wrote Addams, "to find that we possessed a fine illustration of the honesty and kindliness of our new neighbors."

The success of Addams's first 24 hours at Hull House was to be a portent for the rest of her life there. She stayed for nearly 40 years, developing the house into a center for infant care, youth clubs, workers' groups, reading and citizenship classes—a whole range of programs to help the poor find hope, self-respect, and more decent lives. Hull House would come to stand for caring and fairness in every aspect of human activity, and Addams herself would become one of the best-known and most-admired women in the world.

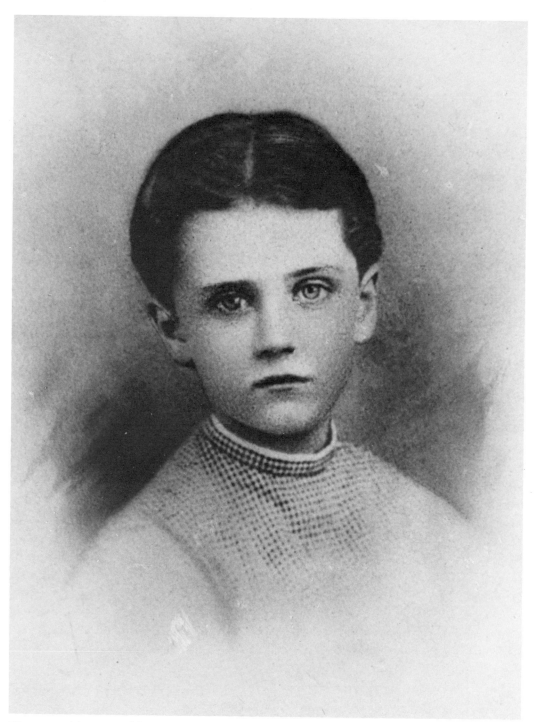

Six-year-old Jane Addams, motherless from the age of two, was strongly attached to her father. She never forgot his advice: "Be honest with yourself inside."

TWO

Above All, "Mental Integrity"

Jane Addams was born on September 6, 1860, the eighth child of a prominent family in the small town of Cedarville, Illinois. Of the nine children born to her parents, John and Sarah Addams, only four would reach maturity. Pregnant with her ninth child at the age of 49, Sarah Addams died in 1863, leaving 2-year-old Jane, 10-year-old James Weber and 3 older daughters—Mary, Martha, and Alice. Five years after Sarah's death, John Addams married Anna Haldeman, a widow from nearby Freeport who had two sons, 18-year-old Henry and 7-year-old George.

Jane welcomed the arrival of George, who was almost the same age as she, but she resented her new stepmother at first. The little girl was used to being pampered by her older siblings and the family servants, and she was taken aback by Anna Addams's unfamiliar habits. The new Mrs. Addams was determined to enforce order in the somewhat unruly household, and she had a quick temper. When she arrived in her new home, she began at once to reorganize it, insisting on formal meal-time behavior, scrupulously orderly rooms, and strict discipline among the children.

Anna Addams was, however, intelligent, cultivated, and basically kind. An avid reader and a talented musician, she often entertained the youngsters by reading plays and novels aloud to them, playing the guitar, and singing folk songs. The children soon became accustomed to her ways, and after a

John Addams, highly respected for his scrupulous honesty and good judgment, was known to his neighbors as "the king gentleman of the district."

few months she won the hearts of both Jane and her siblings. Anna also earned a reputation as an exceptionally gracious hostess, often inviting her husband's friends and business associates to join the family for evenings of music and conversation.

Although Jane grew fond of "Ma," as she began to call her stepmother, she continued to look to her father and her sister Martha for advice and approval. When Martha suddenly died of typhoid fever at the age of 16, 5-year-old Jane became more dependent than ever on her adored father.

John Addams was highly regarded by his neighbors for his honesty, generosity, and quiet religious faith. Born in Pennsylvania, he and his first wife had moved to Illinois in 1844, when he was 22. He built a small gristmill on the banks of Cedar Creek, later investing in land, railroads, banks, and insurance companies. By the time his daughter Jane was born, he was one of the wealthiest men in his community.

In 1854 Addams was elected to the Illinois State Senate, where he became the friend of another Illinois politician of note: Abraham Lincoln. When Addams, who had been reelected to the State Senate seven times, declined to run for an eighth term in 1870, a local newspaper editor observed that "the district might as well go into mourning politically."

Addams was celebrated for his good judgment and the soundness of his opinions. Neighbors liked to tell the story of a farmer who was seen in Cedarville one icy winter day with his ears uncovered. Friends told him if he did not cover his head he would freeze his ears. "No I won't," the farmer reportedly replied. "I just saw John Addams and he says 'taint cold." Her father's reputation for honor was a source of great pride to Jane. She liked to quote a Chicago newspaper editor who once said that although there were probably many legislators who had refused to accept bribes during the Civil War, he knew only one man—

Elm trees shade the brick house in Cedarville, Illinois, where Jane Addams was born and grew up. The Addams family was among the town's wealthiest.

John Addams—who had never even been *offered* a bribe "because bad men were instinctively afraid of him."

Jane Addams would come to be deeply respected for her own honesty, which she credited to her father's influence. In her autobiography she wrote about one "horrid night" when she lay sleepless in bed, tossing and turning because she had told a lie during the day. "My only method of obtaining relief," she recalled, "was to go downstairs to my father's room and make full confession."

Terrified of the dark, the little girl crept downstairs, where she was "faced with the awful necessity of passing the front door—which my father,

because of his Quaker tendencies, did not lock—and of crossing the wide and black expanse of the living room in order to reach his door." At last, trembling and breathless, she reached her father's bedside and revealed her "sin."

Awakened from a deep sleep, John Addams considered the case gravely. Finally, reported his daughter, he said that "if he had a little girl who told lies, he was very glad that she felt too bad to go to sleep afterwards." Jane then "went back to bed as bold as a lion, and slept, if not the sleep of the just, at least that of the comforted."

John Addams was a busy man. A mill owner, banker, and insurance company executive, he was also in-

Illinois lawyer Abraham Lincoln addresses a jury in 1857. Jane Addams treasured Lincoln's letters to her father, whom he addressed as "My Dear Double-D'ed Addams."

volved with such local civic organizations as the school, church, library, and cemetery, all of which he had helped organize. Despite the constant demands of his active life, however, he always seemed to have time for his daughter. When she asked thoughtful questions about the subjects she heard adults talking about, he paid her the compliment of taking them seriously.

She never forgot the spring day in 1865 when she saw that the gateposts outside her home were draped in black-edged American flags. She rushed inside to ask why. "To my amazement," she wrote later, "I found my father in tears, something I had never seen before, having assumed, as all children do, that grown-up people never cried."

Taking his four-year-old daughter on his lap, Addams explained that Abraham Lincoln was dead, the victim of an assassin's bullet. "The two flags, my father's tears, and his impressive statement that the greatest man in the world had died," wrote Addams, "constituted my initiation . . . into the thrill-

Mourners accompany Lincoln's body through Chicago in 1865. The president's death left John Addams in tears, a sight that deeply impressed four-year-old Jane.

ing and solemn interests of a world lying quite outside the two white gateposts."

Her father's patient explanations of world affairs gave Addams what she later called "a valuable possession, a sense of the genuine relationship which may exist between men who share large hopes and like desires." Addams's reference to "men who share large hopes" fits in with her youthful admiration of exclusively male role models. Although Susan B. Anthony and other pioneering femi-

nists had been denouncing women's legal and social inequality for a generation, Addams, as Allen F. Davis notes in his biography, *American Heroine*, seemed "to have had no heroines while growing up.... She had only heroes—[American essayist Ralph Waldo] Emerson, [British philosopher and historian Thomas] Carlyle, [Italian revolutionist Giuseppe] Mazzini, and her father."

A frail child, Jane was often ill. Her most serious ailment, diagnosed as tuberculosis of the spine, left her with a slightly curved back and a pigeon-toed walk. Although people who knew her described her as a pretty, "dreamy-looking" child, she referred to herself as painfully plain. She was even worried that strangers would misjudge her "handsome father" if they realized that he "owned this homely little girl."

Addams later recalled the way she had felt on Sundays, when her father taught a Bible class in the local church. "To my eyes," she wrote in her autobiography, "he was a most imposing figure in his Sunday frock coat, his fine head rising high above all the others. . . . I prayed with all my heart that the ugly, pigeon-toed little girl, whose crooked back obliged her to walk with her head held very much upon one side, would never be pointed out . . . as the daughter of this fine man." To make sure, wrote Addams, she would walk to church next to an uncle; that way, she believed, no one would "identify an Ugly Duckling with her imposing parent."

In her autobiography, Addams recalled a Sunday when she was eight years old: "Arrayed in a new cloak, gorgeous beyond anything I had ever worn before, I stood before my father for his approval." John Addams conceded that the new cloak was "much prettier than any cloak the other little girls in the Sunday school had," but he advised his daughter to wear her old one instead. It would, he said, keep her just as warm, "with the added advantage of not making the other little girls feel badly."

After thinking over his remarks, she asked him what else could be done about inequality among people. He replied that "it might never be righted so far as clothes went, but that people might be equal in things that mattered much more than clothes, the affairs of education and religion, for instance . . . and that it was very stupid to wear the sort of clothes that made it harder to have equality even there." Working among the poor in later life, Jane Addams would remember her father's words.

When she was about 10 years old, he offered another piece of advice she never forgot. Puzzled by remarks she had overheard about foreordination—a religious doctrine asserting that people's spiritual fates are determined before their birth—she asked her father to explain it. She recalled that she had "no doubt that he could make it quite clear."

His answer surprised her. He said he could not explain it, that he doubted that either he or she had the kind of mind that would ever understand it, and that it was, furthermore, not worth worrying about. He told her that it was not important "whether one understood foreordination or not, but that it was very important not to pretend to understand what you didn't understand." What really mattered, he said, was to "be honest with yourself inside,

Like many 19th-century women, Jane Addams selected only men as role models. Among her heroes were (clockwise from top left) Italian patriot Giuseppe Mazzini, American philosopher Ralph Waldo Emerson, and British historian Thomas Carlyle.

whatever happened." John Addams's advice about holding "mental integrity above everything else" was, said Jane Addams later, the most valuable he ever gave her.

Jane Addams's childhood was not, of course, all deep thought and moral lessons. Children growing up in rural Cedarville could roam freely, climbing the pine-forested hills around the vil-lage and splashing in its millstream. Day after summer day, Jane and her stepbrother George played in the fields, picked flowers, explored caves, built forts, and went on imaginary ex-peditions. They collected black wal-nuts, fished in the stream, and hunted snakes. In the winter they ice-skated or played chess and checkers by the fire.

Jane and George also liked to visit

her father's gristmill. It was, she recalled, "full of dusky, floury places which we adored, of empty bins in which we might play house; it had a basement, with piles of bran which were almost as good as sand to play in." At the lumber mill, even greater excitement awaited. There Jane and George sometimes rode the great logs as they moved toward the distant saw blade, imagining with a delicious sense of danger the "sudden, gory death" that awaited them if they failed to jump off in time.

Encouraged by their parents, Jane and George spent much of their time reading. George liked books about science and nature, but Jane's tastes ran to fiction. She was especially fond of the novels of Charles Dickens ("He never wrote anything stupid," she wrote in her journal) and Louisa May Alcott; *Little Women*, she noted, "never seems to grow old." Because John Addams thought novels less instructive than history, he bribed his daughter to read history. Sample rates were a nickel for each of *Plutarch's Lives* and a quarter for each volume of Washington Irving's *Life of Washington*.

John and Anna Addams did not believe in sheltering children from reality, even when it was sorrowful. One winter night when Jane was 15, she was at home alone when word came that an old family friend was dying. She left the warm, lamplit house, hitched up the horse and buggy, and

Anna Addams is flanked by her son George and stepdaughter Jane, both 16 years old in this photograph. The youngsters had grown up as inseparable companions.

rode four miles through a blizzard to the elderly woman's lonely farmhouse. Jane listened to the storm howling outside as she sat with her old friend. "Suddenly the great change came," she recalled of the moment the old woman died. "In place of the face familiar from my earliest childhood . . . there lay upon the pillow strange, august features, stern and withdrawn from all the small affairs of life."

Addams later remembered that, as she drove home through the snow, "the wind from the trees seemed laden with a passing soul, and the riddle of life and death pressed hard; once to be young, to grow old and to die, everything came to that!" Much later, Addams wrote to "protest against the efforts, so often made, to shield chil-

28

dren and young people from all that has to do with death and sorrow." Young people, she asserted, often resent "being denied the common human experiences. They too wish to climb steep stairs." Children were cheated, she said, when they were kept from sorrow, just as they would be cheated if they were kept from joy.

At the age of 16, Addams was an attractive young woman. Of average height for her generation (five feet, three inches) and slender (95 pounds), she had long, brown hair and wide, dark eyes. Nevertheless, she retained her childhood doubts about her appearance; describing herself in a letter to a cousin she had never met, she said her nose expressed "no character whatever, and contains eight freckles horrible to relate (I counted them this morning)."

Jane, however, was no longer a child; she would soon graduate from high school. College was the exception rather than the rule for women in the 1870s, but John Addams approved of higher education for women, and Jane wanted to go. In 1877, 17 years old and very excited, she boarded a train at the Cedarville station, waved good-bye to her family, and set off for Rockford Seminary, a "female college" in Rockford, Illinois.

Although she was considered attractive by other Rockford Seminary students, Addams thought of herself as an "ugly duckling" with a "characterless" nose.

THREE

"Becoming Someone"

Before the Civil War, which ended in 1865, only a handful of colleges, among them Vassar in New York State, Mount Holyoke in Massachusetts, and Oberlin in Ohio, offered degrees to women. As late as 1877, when Jane Addams graduated from high school, many Americans still thought education for women was unnecessary—even dangerous. "Must we crowd education on our daughters, and for the sake of having them 'intellectual' make them puny, nervous, and their whole earthly existence a struggle between life and death?" asked one educator.

Another, a professor at Harvard Medical School, published a book "proving" that higher education damaged women's reproductive systems. The author of an article in the popular *Scribner's Monthly* magazine stated that women's colleges bred "diseases

of body, diseases of imagination, vices of body and imagination—everything we would save our children from."

John Addams thought such views were nonsense and so did his daughter Jane. Still, when she arrived at Rockford Seminary, she felt she was doing something unusual and rather daring. One of her fellow freshmen later recorded her first impression of Addams: "A little girl with very pretty, light brown hair, pushed back, and particularly direct, earnest eyes; but she looked as I knew I was feeling, very trembly inside."

Like the 22 other women in her freshman class, Addams felt singled out for special opportunity, and she was determined to make the most of it. She and her friends, she recalled, "really believed" the words they framed and hung on the wall of their chess club: "There is the same difference between the learned and the unlearned as there is between the living and the dead."

The avowed purpose of Rockford Seminary, which had been established in 1851 by the Illinois Presbyterian and Congregationalist churches, was to combine domestic and religious training and to promote "purity," "submissiveness," and "domesticity" in its female students. "The chief end of women's education," announced the school's first principal, "is not simply to shine in society, but to elevate and purify and adorn the home."

Rockford's schedules and discipline were strict. After rising at 6:30, students filed into the dining hall for breakfast, where they remained standing until the principal gave the signal to sit. They were expected to call one another "Miss," even in private. The students attended daily chapel, weekly prayer meetings, Sunday services, and religion classes. They exercised for an hour each day by walking around and around the school buildings, they tended the woodstoves that heated their rooms, and they washed their own dishes and linen.

Addams quickly became one of the most popular students at Rockford. "Even at this stage of her life," notes biographer Allen Davis, "there seems to have been something about her that attracted all kinds of people." Addams's room was "an available refuge from all perplexities," recalled one friend. "There was always something 'doing' where she was," remembered another, who added, "However mopey it might be elsewhere there was intellectual ozone in her vicinity." Among Addams's closest friends was Ellen Starr, a witty and artistic young woman from the small town of Durand, Illinois. After a year at Rockford, Starr left to teach school, but she and Addams would remain friends for the rest of their lives.

The young women of Rockford were encouraged either to marry or to become missionaries who would carry Western culture and Christianity to such "unenlightened" nations as China. When they left school, most of the students chose one or the other of these alternatives. Addams, however, had other ideas. She was not yet sure what she wanted to do with her life, but she knew one thing: She wanted to work, to succeed, and to "become someone."

During a debate in her junior year, Addams said: "The impervious will of man is at last forced to admit that woman, like himself, possesses an intellect and that she exerts a potent influence in the age in which she lives.... She wishes not to be a man, nor like a man, but she claims the same right to independent thought and action."

These were daring words for a woman of Addams's generation and

College women perform physics experiments in the late 19th century. Many Americans thought such activities posed a threat to their daughters.

economic class. For such women, the "proper" career was marriage; "independent thought and action" were not considered appropriate goals. Whether they were married or not, poor women worked in Addams's day just as they always had, but when a middle- or upper-class woman decided to pursue a career, it meant she had no plans to marry.

Addams enjoyed playing with her sister Mary's children, but she did not envy Mary. Marriage versus "becoming someone"? Addams made her choice and gave no evidence of ever regretting it. As for missionary work, it apparently never entered her mind, despite the pressure put on the Rockford students to follow that course.

Addams knew what she did not want: marriage or life as a missionary. She also knew what she did want: a real college degree. Rockford had never offered its graduates more than a certificate attesting to their years in school, but Addams wanted to receive a bachelor of arts degree just as college-educated men did. She therefore designed her program of studies to meet the qualifications for a degree at nearby Beloit College for men.

During her four years at Rockford,

Thomas De Quincey, author of a popular book about "opium eating," inspired Addams and her friends to try the drug. The experiment was not a success.

she took courses in German, Latin, Greek, history, literature, algebra, and trigonometry. She also studied science—geology, chemistry, mineralogy, and astronomy—as well as music, philosophy, and Bible history. She proved to be an outstanding student; most of her grades ranged between 9.5 and 10, which was perfect.

Addams and her friends worked hard, but, like students everywhere, they sometimes found school unbearably dull. "So much of our time is spent in preparation, so much in routine, and so much in sleep, we find it difficult to have any experience at all," complained Addams in her sophomore year. The future humanitarian also noted that she and her group did not always "tamely accept such a state of affairs," instead, engaging in "various and restless attempts to break through" the monotony of life at Rockford.

One day, she reported in her autobiography, she and four friends were discussing British author Thomas De Quincey's famous 1821 book, *Confessions of an English Opium Eater*. Although De Quincey graphically described the horrors of his opium addiction, the young women were curious. "Recreational" drug use was almost unheard of at this period, and Addams and her friends had never been instructed about its potential for danger. They decided to take opium, as the poet had, in order to understand his work "more sympathetically." Without explaining how they obtained the drug, Addams wrote that they "solemnly consumed small white powders at intervals" throughout one Sunday afternoon.

The young women had hoped their experiment would give them new insights about life, but the results were disappointing. "No mental reorientation took place, and the suspense and excitement did not even permit us to grow sleepy," noted Addams. Drug abuse was not a recognized problem among the students of Addams's day, but still, five young women ingesting opium on campus did not calculate their activity to please Rockford's stern administrators.

When one of the teachers found out what was going on, she gave each of the experimenters an emetic (medicine that causes vomiting), and ordered them to go to their rooms. They were, said the teacher firmly, "to appear at family worship after supper whether [they] were able to or not." So much, thought Addams, for gaining a "sympathetic understanding of human experience" through drugs.

Fortunately, more conventional forms of amusement were also available at Rockford. With her classmates, Addams organized a chess club, a debating society, and an amateur theatrical group. She also edited and wrote for the *Rockford Seminary Magazine*. On weekends, she often took friends to visit her family in Cedarville, which was only two hours away by train. Here, Anna Addams would play her guitar and sing to her stepdaughter and her schoolmates. On other weekends, young men from Beloit College came to call and, in the winter, to take Rockford women sleighriding—properly chaperoned, of course.

The Beloit men also came to seek wives. During the time Addams was at Rockford, 16 of her classmates left school to marry Beloit students. Ad-

Graduates carry Vassar's traditional daisy chain in 1908. Founded in 1861, the Poughkeepsie, New York, institution was among the nation's first women's colleges.

dams's nephew, James Weber Linn, reported in his 1935 biography, *Jane Addams*, that his aunt received a proposal of marriage from Rollin Salisbury, one of Beloit's outstanding students and the president of his class. Predictably, Addams refused him, and Salisbury, said Linn, "remained a bachelor all his days."

On her visits to Cedarville, Addams had many long talks with her father. Although he considered marriage the proper life for a woman, he finally came to understand that it was not the answer for his daughter. With his approval, she decided to enter the Women's Medical College of Philadelphia after she graduated from Rockford in the spring of 1881. Although she did

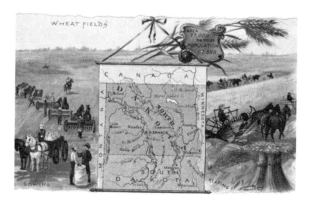

Jane Addams's inheritance from her father included 80 acres of land in the sparsely populated but extremely fertile Dakota Territory.

not envision medicine as a career, she believed that medical school would occupy her mind and give her some useful skills while she was thinking about her true vocation.

Addams had been out of college only a few weeks when she experienced what she later called "the greatest sorrow that can ever come to me." During an August family vacation in northern Wisconsin, John Addams, then 59 years old, was exploring the rugged countryside when he suddenly became ill. His wife and daughter rushed him to a hospital, but they were too late; his appendix had ruptured. Within hours, John Addams was dead.

The death of her father left Jane Addams desolate. She felt, she told her friend Ellen Starr, "purposeless" and "without ambition." She tried to dull her despair by writing a brief memoir of her father. "He was the uncompromising enemy of wrong and wrong doing," it said in part. "He was a leader as well as a safe and fearless advocate of right things in public life. My own vivid recollection of John H. Addams is the fact that he was a man of purest and sternest integrity."

John Addams left his wife and four surviving children a substantial estate. Jane inherited a 247-acre farm and 60 acres of timberland in Illinois, 80 acres of land in the Dakota Territory, and shares of stock worth about $60,000—a considerable fortune in the 1880s. Without financial worries, but still in deep mourning, Jane Addams carried out her plan to attend the Women's Medical College in Philadelphia, largely because she had told her father she would.

She enrolled in October 1881, but she soon realized that medical school was not for her. She found herself incapable of concentrating on her classes, an "utter failure" and unable "to work at the best of myself," as she wrote in her journal. In spite of her self-criticism, Addams received high grades in her first semester. Still, she felt alienated, "growing more sullen and less sympathetic every day." What she saw as her failure to shine as a medical student troubled her deeply. "People expect certain things of me," she wrote gloomily. "I have every chance to obtain them and yet fall far short."

As students look on, Women's Medical College doctors operate on a patient in the 1880s. Addams dropped out of the Philadelphia school after one semester.

In February 1882, she dropped out of school and entered a hospital, suffering from severe back pain as well as depression. That April she underwent an operation to straighten her spine. Perhaps, she thought, she could conquer her emotional troubles once her physical pain had been cured.

The operation was a major one; after the surgery she had to lie flat on her back for six months. When her doctor finally allowed her to get up, he fitted her with a kind of corset to support her healing spine. Made of leather, whalebone, and steel, the device made it hard for her to breathe, but she wore it uncomplainingly for a year. "I have had the kindest care," she wrote to a friend about her convalescence, "and am emerging with a straight back and a fresh hold on life and endeavor, I hope."

Despite her optimistic words, she was slow to regain her vitality. In a letter to Ellen Starr in the spring of 1883, she wrote: "It seems quite essential for the establishment of my health and temper that I have a radical change, and so I have accepted the advice given to every exhausted American, 'Go abroad.'"

In August, Addams, her stepmother,

A ruined Scottish castle is framed by Loch Ness, one of the sites Addams visited in 1883. Strenuous hiking around Europe greatly improved her health.

and four other women sailed for Europe. Tramping through the mountains of Scotland and Germany, climbing the steep stairs of museums and cathedrals in England, France, and Italy, and riding trains across Europe proved excellent therapy, and Addams soon discarded her painful back brace for good. She even gained much-needed weight.

Addams's European tour improved her health and expanded her cultural horizons. Even more important, however, was what it showed her about a

side of life she had never known. A few months after the American women crossed the Atlantic, she and her companions found themselves in London. There, Addams recalled in her autobiography, she "received an ineradicable impression" of the "wretchedness" of the poor. Escorted by a tour guide to the slums of east London, the group saw crowds of poor residents bidding on spoiled vegetables discarded by city grocers.

"At the end of a dingy street lighted by only occasional flares of gas," recalled Addams, "we saw two huge masses of ill-clad people clamoring around two hucksters' carts.... They were huddled into ill-fitting, cast-off clothing.... Their pale faces were dominated by ... the cunning and shrewdness of the bargain-hunter who starves if he cannot make a successful trade." Addams's strongest impression, she said, was of hands, "myriads of hands, empty, pathetic, nerveless and workworn, showing white in the uncertain light of the street, and clutching forward for food which was already unfit to eat.

"I have never since been able to see a number of hands held upward," she said, "even ... when they belong to a class of chubby children who wave them in eager response to a teacher's query, without a certain revival of this memory, a clutching of the heart reminiscent of the despair and resentment which seized me then."

After her visit to the East End, Addams "went about London furtively [stealthily], afraid to look down narrow streets and alleys lest they disclose again this hideous human need, bewildered that the world should be going on as usual." Her world, she realized, did not expect her even to remember

Ragged slum-dwellers crowd a London street. Addams longed to eliminate such "wretchedness," but in 1885 she had no idea of how to go about it.

these people's misery, much less do anything about it.

Well-off and free to do as she chose, Addams nevertheless felt trapped. She knew she wanted to help people, but how? The more she saw of Europe's cultural riches and the squalor of its slums, factories, and mines, the less she was able to see a clear path toward serving humanity. "After almost two years," reported her nephew, "she returned to Cedarville spiritually more confused than when she had left it."

Chicago immigrant families work on sewing projects "farmed out" by a local factory. Addams was astonished by the crowded conditions she saw in the city's slums.

FOUR

"A Cathedral of Humanity"

Still perplexed about her role in life, Jane Addams returned to the United States from Europe in the summer of 1885. She spent much of the next two years in Baltimore with her stepmother. "I seemed," she wrote of this period, "to have reached the nadir [low point] of my nervous depression and sense of maladjustment." She wrote a few essays about her European trip for the *Rockford Seminary Magazine*, studied the art books she had brought back, went to concerts, lectures, and parties, and reread the journals she had kept during her trip abroad. She also organized an art club for women and took drawing lessons.

None of these activities lifted her spirits. She wrote the words of a popular hymn in her journal, ruefully observing that they applied to her: "Weary of myself and sick of asking/

What I am and what I ought to be." Addams was intelligent, creative, and well educated—but she had no work to do, no responsibilities, and no specific goals.

Finally, she decided to go back to Europe, this time with Ellen Starr and several other friends. After her graduation from Rockford Seminary, Addams had become an active alumna, frequently making contributions to its library and other facilities. The mission she assigned herself and Starr on their European trip was the acquisition of art reproductions for the school. The group arrived in England just before Christmas, 1887.

Now 27 years old, Addams felt much more independent than she had on her first journey abroad. "I am quite impressed with the difference in my age and dignity between this trip to

Ulm's magnificent cathedral, which displayed the symbols of many faiths, made a deep impression on Addams when she visited Germany in 1888.

case, the "simple plan" took definite shape on this trip.

Before she saw the Madrid bullfight that crystallized her plan, Addams visited the German city of Ulm. She was filled with awe by the city's vast cathedral, where carvings and statues illustrated the history of humanity's quest for spiritual enlightenment. Addams wrote that she was "startled" to discover that the church "contained Greek philosophers as well as Hebrew prophets, and [that] among the disciples and saints stood the discoverer of music and a builder of pagan temples."

Gazing around the magnificent house of worship, she envisioned a "cathedral of humanity" that would be "capacious enough to house a fellowship of common purpose," and "beautiful enough to persuade men to hold fast to the vision of human solidarity." These thoughts, wrote Addams, were the seeds of her philosophy for Hull House, where "those of widely differing religious beliefs" could work together in peace and harmony.

From Germany, Addams went to Spain by way of Italy and France; after the Madrid bullfight and her visit to London in 1888, she returned to the United States, where she would begin to turn her ideas into reality.

In January 1889, Addams and Starr moved into a boardinghouse in Chicago. Their first step was to round up support for what they had begun to call "the scheme." Addams intended

Europe and the one before," she wrote humorously to her sister Mary. "Then I was Mademoiselle and Fraulein [French and German for "Miss"] and I felt like a young girl." This time, she said, she felt "dignified" because everyone called her *Madame.*

In her autobiography, Addams wrote, "It is hard to tell just when the very simple plan which afterward developed into the Settlement [Hull House] began to form itself in my mind. It may have been even before I went to Europe for the second time." In any

Ellen Starr, whose close friendship with Addams started at Rockford Seminary, played an essential role in the establishment of Hull House.

to use her inheritance to pay most of the expenses, but she hoped to get both moral and financial support from Chicago's religious establishment. She became a member of the Fourth Presbyterian Church, attending Bible lectures and teaching a Sunday-school class. Fourth Presbyterian's congregation included some of Chicago's wealthiest and most influential people, some of them interested in philanthropy (helping the needy).

Whenever Addams met these people, she told them about her plans for a settlement house. She tirelessly repeated her principal argument: "A house, easily accessible, ample in space, hospitable and tolerant in spirit, situated in the midst of the large foreign colonies which so easily isolate themselves in American cities, would be in itself a serviceable thing for Chicago."

Addams also emphasized her theory that "the dependence of classes on each other is reciprocal," meaning that the well-to-do people who helped the poor would also benefit themselves. Her proposals, she wrote later, generally "received courteous attention, and the discussion, while often skeptical, was always friendly."

Starr, too, actively pursued support for the settlement house. After leaving Rockford Seminary, she had taught at the Kirkland School, one of Chicago's most fashionable academies for young women. She had met the parents of many of her affluent students, and now she called on them, spreading the word about the project Addams had envisioned.

Starr later recalled the "conversion" of one of Chicago's most popular clergymen, Frank Gunsaulus, pastor of Chicago's Plymouth Congregational Church. When she and Addams met him, he was extremely doubtful about their plan. He had run across a number of wealthy, well-meaning, but impractical "young ladies" who wished to "deal with the poor," but had no idea

At first, clergyman Frank Gunsaulus was skeptical about the idea of a settlement house, but he soon became one of Hull House's strongest supporters.

of how to proceed. He suspected he had just met two more, but Addams and Starr proved to be different.

They explained that they meant business; the establishment they wanted to operate would not be run for the entertainment of part-time "charity ladies," but for immigrants who badly needed help. They did not intend to found "an institution," they said, but a house where they could live among the poor, learning about their needs from experience.

"Good!" said Gunsaulus. "The King-

dom of Heaven isn't an organization or an institution." After advising the women to stay away from people who "form committees" and from those who go out "harpooning for souls," he promised to spread the word about their project among his parishioners.

Addams and Starr talked with other prominent clergymen, too. Many said they would offer money and moral support when needed. With much of the city's religious establishment behind them, the women set about learning how they could run the project they had in mind. They visited Chicago's leading charitable organizations, including the Armour Mission, the Chicago Woman's Club, the Women's Christian Temperance Union, and the Association of Collegiate Alumnae.

These groups responded with enthusiasm—sometimes, felt Addams, with too much enthusiasm. Officials at the Armour Mission, an educational institution for the poor, urged the women to establish their settlement house near its own headquarters; Armour, they said, could help manage the new project.

"I am very much against that, and Jane says she is too," said Starr in a letter to her sister. "We should simply be swallowed up in a great organization." The woman's club, too, wanted to sponsor the new settlement house, but Addams was determined to keep the project independent of all official organizations. Starr, who always re-

Addams discovered this mansion on Chicago's Halsted Street in May 1889. By September she had turned it into the pioneering project known as Hull House.

ferred to the settlement house as "Jane's idea," agreed with her friend as usual.

Addams knew she needed to learn more about Chicago and its inhabitants before opening the settlement house. When she was not visiting charitable institutions, reading about social movements in Europe, or writing letters and giving speeches about her plan, she was busily investigating the city. She trudged tirelessly through some of its worst slums, observing and talking to immigrant residents.

These expeditions gave her a new kind of education. After she visited south Chicago's Italian section, she wrote: "It was exactly as if we were in a quarter of Naples or Rome; the parents and children spoke nothing but Italian and dressed like Italian peasants. They were more crowded than I imagined people ever lived in America, four families for instance of seven or eight each living in one room for which they paid eleven dollars a month, and constantly afraid of being ejected.... They never begged or even complained."

It was during one of these walking tours, on a spring day in 1889, that Addams and Starr discovered the building that would one day be famous as Hull House. The two-story brick structure, shabby but sound, stood between a funeral parlor and a saloon.

Despite its dreary setting, the house appealed to Addams at once. Set back from Halsted Street, it had a broad porch on three sides, handsome wooden pillars, and what Addams called "a gracious aspect." As soon as she laid eyes on it, she inquired about renting it.

The owner of the house, Helen Culver, was doubtful about these prospective tenants. Why would two women, obviously educated and well-to-do, want to rent a house in a run-down area of Chicago? After Addams explained what they wanted to do with the house, however, Culver relented and gave her a lease. Filled with excitement, Addams and Starr began to renovate and furnish their new home.

"The fine old house responded kindly to repairs," noted Addams. Investigating the building's history, she learned that the previous tenants had always kept a pitcher of water on the top staircase. When she asked why, a neighbor explained: The attic contained a ghost, and a ghost, as everybody knew, could not cross water. Addams was amused rather than

A Hull House neighbor offers a shy wave to a passing photographer. Addams was particularly concerned about the welfare of the area's children.

frightened by the tale. On September 18, 1889, after several months of repairing and decorating, Addams and Starr moved into their new home. They named it Hull House, after its original owner.

The area's residents, most of them poor Italian immigrants, were suspicious of the newcomers at first.

The shacks that housed much of Chicago's immigrant population were steamy in summer, icy in winter, and always in danger of burning to the ground.

Wealthy women, after all, did not often visit this part of town, much less come to live in it. Eager to win their neighbors' confidence, Addams and Starr decided to demonstrate their respect for Italian culture. After decorating the walls of Hull House with photographs they had taken in Italy the year before, they invited the whole neighborhood to a "reading party."

At the party, they read aloud from *Romola*, a George Eliot novel about humanitarianism. The story takes place in Italy, and Addams, who spoke Italian fluently, read the book in that language. The guests at Hull House that first evening were astonished by everything they saw and heard. Addams later recalled seeing one man shaking his head as he said that the evening was "the strangest thing he had met in his experience."

Hull House was known to many Chicagoans even before it opened. Addams, an effective public speaker and a good organizer, had attracted attention among the city's most influential people. Furthermore, she made good copy for reporters and writers. She was attractive, wealthy, educated, and about to embark on a project very unusual for its time. Newspapers and magazines had run frequent stories in the spring and summer of 1889, almost all of them highly complimentary.

Starr played an important role in the establishment of Hull House, but she refused to take any credit. "I am un-

An immigrant family makes artificial flowers at home. Because the rate paid for "piecework" was extremely low, such workers often put in 16-hour days.

willing," she said to one friend in a letter, "to let people suppose that I would have worked it out." In any case, it was Addams who had taken the lead and Addams who was the subject of public interest.

Reporters called her "a young lady of independent means and generous culture," and characterized her as the "physical expression of modest simplicity itself." Many writers praised Addams's "wonderful spirituality," which both amused and annoyed her. After the publication of one such description of herself, she complained to Starr that she was getting tired of so many people "peering into my face to detect spirituality."

Wary of Hull House in the beginning,

neighbors gradually learned to trust the two strange but kind women who appeared so anxious to help them. Crowds of local residents, many of them women with babies and young children, began to visit. Realizing that one of the community's most urgent needs was a nursery school, Addams called on Jenny Dow, a young and wealthy woman who had volunteered her services. Dow started a kindergarten class, enrolling 24 children and paying all the expenses herself.

Dow was followed by half a dozen young men and women from Chicago's "best families"; by the end of the year 20 volunteers lived at Hull House, and others reported in on a daily or weekly basis. Some of the socially prominent women came to the settlement only because they were curious or because working with the poor was fashionable. Many of them, however, sincerely wanted to help and became loyal and indispensable aides.

The unpaid volunteers who lived at Hull House did their own laundry, cooking, cleaning, and house maintenance. They all worked long, hard hours; in Hull House's first year, 50,000 people came through its doors. The idealistic young workers were inspired both by the needs of the people they served and by Jane Addams herself.

One of the volunteers from the early years recalled that "Miss Addams was able to appreciate others' points of view without necessarily agreeing with

Mary Rozet Smith, a young, well-educated Chicago socialite, was one of the first Hull House volunteers. She and Addams became lifelong friends.

them, and without coercing others toward her own [opinions]." Another resident said that Addams "had the power to value human beings, to appreciate them, and to feel in terms of them." Still another observed that it was Addams's "genuine freedom of mind and friendliness of spirit" that had "made Hull House possible."

The enthusiasm of these volunteers confirmed Addams's belief that wealthy young people wanted and needed useful work to do. Through Hull House, she meant to assist not only the poor but also rich, educated young men and women who were bored and frustrated by inactivity, just as she had been a few years earlier. She knew from experience that no one is more miserable than an individual whose life is full of luxury but empty of purpose.

Addams herself now had more than enough to do. Her neighbors had learned that when she said she was there to help them, she meant exactly that. As James Linn noted in his biography, "It was obvious that if you went to the House you were welcome; if you called, you were called upon; and if you let the young women know there was anything they could do for you, they did it if they could." Addams, said Linn, "washed new-born babies, and minded children, and nursed the sick, and prepared the dead for burial as naturally as any woman of the neighborhood did for her friends. She had more friends, that was all."

Addams made herself available at all hours of the day and night, venturing into "bad" sections of the city, confident that no one would harm her. One dark night she received word that a woman on a far-off street was having her first baby alone. The mother-to-be, Addams was told, was not married, and no neighborhood woman would "touch the likes of her." It was three o'clock in the morning, and Addams had never witnessed childbirth. Nevertheless, she threw on her coat, hurried to the woman's side, and safely delivered the baby.

She proved her courage in many ways. One night she was awakened by a noise; in the dim light she saw a strange man in her room. Thinking of her young nephew, who was sleeping in the next room, she whispered, "Don't make a noise." When the intruder dashed toward the open window, Addams sat up in bed. "You'll be hurt if you go that way," she said firmly. "Go down by the stairs and let yourself out." Meekly, the astonished burglar did as he was told.

Months later she discovered another would-be robber in the house. When she calmly asked him what he thought he was doing, he managed to blurt out his story. He was not a professional burglar, he said, but an unemployed laborer with a hungry family, and he had become desperate. She told him to go home and come back in the morning. Not knowing what to expect, the housebreaker nervously presented

Carefully dressed kindergarten pupils arrive at Hull House for a class. Addams regarded child care as one of the community's most pressing needs.

Watched by their supervisors, elderly women stitch clothing in a 19th-century factory. Establishments like this one were known as sweatshops.

himself at Hull House the next day. There he learned that Addams had found him a job.

Addams's life at Hull House, of course, consisted of much more than midnight emergencies. Every morning, the settlement house offered kindergarten for the neighborhood's youngest children and English-language and crafts classes for their mothers. In the afternoons, older children arrived for club meetings, vocational training, and classes in art and music. Evenings featured cultural programs and more classes for adults. Hull House was always seething with activity.

Although she was in charge of the settlement's operations, Addams did not play the role of boss. She worked right along with the other residents, putting in regular 12-hour days as a teacher and employment counselor. She also helped with the housework,

visited neighborhood residents, conferred with the troubled people who came to Hull House for help and advice, and did all the bookkeeping.

There was, in short, no work at Hull House that Jane Addams did not do. Recalling her first day at the settlement House, one long-term volunteer offered a revealing glimpse of its director: "I arrived at Hull House, Chicago, a little before breakfast time, and found there Henry Standing Bear, a Kickapoo Indian, awaiting the front door to be opened. It was Miss Addams who opened it, holding on her left arm a . . . baby belonging to the cook, who was behindhand with breakfast. Miss Addams was a little hindered in her movements by a super energetic kindergarten child, left by its mother while she went to a sweatshop [clothing factory]."

In addition to her day-to-day work

at the settlement house, Addams continued to make frequent speeches, trying to raise funds to supplement the money that she and the other volunteers contributed. Her speeches, which she prepared with great care, were not dramatic, but they were highly effective. "Her most striking characteristic was her extreme simplicity," recalled an admirer who had often heard her lecture. "She has always had the effect of speaking to but one, and that one is each one."

Before she opened Hull House, Addams had been aware of the poverty of Chicago's immigrant population, but until she began to work there, she did not fully understand what it meant to be poor. Two months after the settlement house started operations, she wrote a letter to her stepbrother George. "One is so overpowered by the misery and narrow lives of so large a number of city people," she said, "that the wonder is that conscientious people can let it alone."

Once she started, there was no question about Addams's "letting it alone." She was appalled but not depressed by the wretchedness she saw around her because she believed she could do something to change it. She had found her life's work at last.

Addams produced an endless stream of letters to her stepmother and siblings, and she visited them as often as she could. When family members were in trouble or financial need,

A Hull House volunteer (center) joins Addams (right) and Starr for a tea break. Such quiet moments were rare for the busy settlement-house staff.

she was quick to supply advice and money. Still, there was tension among the group. Her sister Alice, for example, thought Jane should give up her work and come home to care for her stepmother. Anna Addams herself disapproved of her stepdaughter's deep involvement with her work, to which she offered neither moral nor financial support. When Jane Addams remarked that her father, had he lived, would undoubtedly have contributed money to Hull House, the older woman was furious.

Writing to her sister Mary about the rest of the family, Addams said, "I have the most helpless, bewildered feeling about them." She loved them dearly, but she did not give in to their pressure. Hull House and its occupants had become her true home and family.

A trio of fish-market workers lines up for a snapshot. Before child-labor laws were passed, millions of American children worked six-day weeks.

FIVE

A "Salon of Democracy"

Money was always in short supply at Hull House, but Jane Addams proved a skillful financial manager, and the institution never went into debt. Addams paid most of the expenses herself, using both her personal income and the money she earned making speeches. Hull House volunteers contributed funds when they could, and occasionally a wealthy admirer offered a large donation. Cash gifts were normally greeted with cheers at the hard-pressed settlement house, but one would-be benefactor created a serious problem for Addams.

It began with her effort to solve one of the most pressing concerns of the poor: secure housing. Because day laborers were never sure how long their jobs would last, they worried constantly about being evicted from their homes for nonpayment of rent. Partic-

ularly concerned about the living situations of the young "factory girls" who visited Hull House, Addams started an experiment in cooperative housing in 1891. She rented and furnished two large apartments, which she made available to a group of these young working women. Hull House paid the first month's rent; after that, the tenants themselves were responsible for the enterprise.

When the "Jane Club," as the venture was called, proved successful, Addams decided to expand the operation. She wanted to construct a whole apartment building that could be used for working women's cooperative housing. At this point, a Chicago factory owner offered to give Hull House $20,000 with which to build the new "clubhouse." The problem, as Addams later put it, was that the pro-

According to the U.S. Department of Labor, Hull House's cooperative residence for women was the first successful venture of its kind in the nation.

posed donor "was notorious for underpaying the girls in his establishment"; there were, she added ominously, "even darker stories" about him.

The "tainted money" created a dilemma. Addams had publicly announced the need for money to build a working-women's residence; now that it was offered, could she turn it down? And could she blame the factory owner "for that which all of his competitors and his associates consider legitimate"? Finally, she came to a conclusion: "Social changes," she asserted, "can only be inaugurated by those who feel the unrighteousness of contemporary conditions." In that light, she wrote, "It seemed clearly impossible to erect a clubhouse for working girls with such money." She declined the offer.

Fortunately, it was not long before an "old friend of Hull House" who was "much interested in working girls" came forward with funds to build the new cooperative apartment house. When it opened, it, too, operated smoothly. After carefully inspecting it, the head of the U.S. Department of Labor stated that it was the first cooperative residence "founded and managed by women that had ever succeeded in the United States."

The following year, Addams again proved her effectiveness. One day, after she had finished a speech about "sharing opportunity," a young man from the audience came up to speak to her. Introducing himself as William Kent, he said he had been moved by her words and wanted to help. Kent, it seemed, was very wealthy; among his assets was a large parcel of land near Hull House. Built on the land, which Kent had inherited, were a number of decayed and unsafe buildings; several housed brothels.

"You might begin there," suggested Addams. This, recalled Kent later, was not the kind of answer he had expected; he stalked off indignantly. Addams's speech, however, continued to haunt him. Two weeks later, he called at Hull House. "I have decided," he said unsmilingly, "to turn over that property to you to use as you please."

If Kent expected simple gratitude he was mistaken. What Addams said was, "You might tear the buildings down and make the lots a place for the children to play on."

"Do as you please about that," snapped Kent.

"Will you pay for tearing them down?" she asked.

This was too much for Kent. "I don't see why I should!" he roared.

Smiling sweetly, Addams said, "And will you pay the taxes?"

With that, Kent stormed off, shouting over his shoulder, "You ask too much!"

Addams, Kent wrote later, "was the first person who ever forced me to try to think things out. You might say she converted me." A week later he was back at Hull House. "I'll do whatever you say," he said. A few months later, on May 1, 1892, Chicago's first public playground opened its gates. Looking on proudly was the former owner of the playground land, William Kent.

Men and women of all ages came to Hull House for assistance. "We early found ourselves spending many hours in efforts to secure support for deserted women, insurance for bewil-

City children play with the only "toys" available—a handcart and a bundle of rags. Chicago had no public playgrounds until Jane Addams opened one in 1892.

dered widows, damages for injured [workers], furniture from the clutches of the installment store," Addams noted in her autobiography. The relationship "of the Settlement to its neighborhood," she added, "resembles that of the big brother whose mere presence on the playground protects the little one from bullies."

Addams was deeply sympathetic to any helpless person in need of protection, but she was especially concerned about the children of the neighborhood, many of whom lived—and died—in appalling circumstances. "We early learned to know the children of hard-driven mothers who went out to work all day," she recalled. "The first

Tenement-raised Chicago children cautiously explore a new world. Land for the city's first playground was donated by Hull House supporter William Kent.

three crippled children we encountered ... had all been injured while their mothers were at work; one had fallen out of a third-story window, another had been burned, and a third had a curved spine due to the fact that for three years he had been tied all day to the leg of the kitchen table."

Addams found it hard to control her rage over such tragedies. "With all of the efforts made by modern society to nurture and educate the young," she exclaimed, "how stupid it is to permit the mothers of young children to spend themselves in the coarser work of the world!" Obtaining legislation that limited the working hours of women and children would become one of her highest priorities.

Addams was also deeply concerned about what she called "neglected and forlorn old age." She wrote about one "tottering old lady" who was brought to Hull House by a 10-year-old boy. The woman, the boy told Addams, was a stranger to his family, but they had been letting her sleep in their kitchen for the past six weeks because "she had nowhere to go." Noting that "Miss Addams's house" was much bigger than his family's, the boy asked if she would let the woman stay with her.

"The old woman herself said absolutely nothing," recalled Addams, but looked on "with that gripping fear of the poorhouse in her eyes." The "poorhouse," formally known as the County Infirmary, was regarded with horror by the poor—for good reason, as Addams pointed out. "To give an old woman only a chair and a bed, to leave her no cupboard in which her treasures may be stowed," she wrote, "is to reduce living almost beyond the level of human endurance."

Addams found room for the "tottering old lady," but of course, she could not take in all the city's aged poor. What she did do was set up a program for two-week "summer vacations" for poorhouse residents. These lonely people returned to the infirmary after their holidays, said Addams, "with wonderous tales of their adventures with which they regaled [their fellow inmates] during the long winter."

"In spite of the poignant experiences—or perhaps because of them—the memory of the first years at Hull House is more or less blurred with fatigue," wrote Addams in her autobiography, "for we could of course become accustomed only gradually to the unending activity and to the confusion of a house constantly filling and refilling with groups of people."

These crowds came to the settlement house for more than physical necessities; they came to nourish their

An immigrant couple rests after a long day's work. Hull House's elderly neighbors lived in dread of being sent to the County Infirmary, or "poorhouse."

spirits and minds as well. One of the first buildings especially constructed for Hull House was an art gallery, which, noted Addams, "appealed to the powers of enjoyment as over against a wage-earning capacity."

Many of the young volunteers at Hull House were highly knowledgeable about music, painting, and literature. Most had spent considerable time in Europe, where they had learned to appreciate that continent's culture. Assuming that slum dwellers were much like themselves, only without money, these young people were eager to arrange concerts of classical music, lectures by college professors, and art exhibits for their new neighbors.

The poor people who lived nearby did attend these Hull House events, if

Hull House players end a performance with a curtain call. Chicagoans were impressed by the settlement house's polished theatrical productions.

Mothers and children enjoy an outing sponsored by a New Rochelle, New York, settlement house, one of the many institutions inspired by Jane Addams's work.

at first only because they were curious about the house and its residents. But Addams soon realized that Chicago's European immigrants did not need her and her associates to tell them about the culture of their own homelands. They needed, she decided, what their struggle to survive in America had largely taken from them: the chance to enjoy their own culture again; a break from the harshness of their lives.

When the settlement's immigrant neighbors realized that their contributions were welcome at Hull House, many revealed impressive cultural resources. Immigrants from Greece started the the "Plato Club," where they discussed philosophy, and other Greek-Americans took advantage of the Hull House auditorium to present classical plays by Aeschylus and Sophocles. Their performances drew crowds of Chicagoans, astonished by the newcomers' educational polish and dramatic skill. German immigrants staged readings of works by Schiller and Goethe; Italian-born residents met to discuss Dante and Michelangelo.

Recognizing that there were many talented artisans among the local residents, Addams opened a "museum" to display their handiwork. Here visitors could see beautifully wrought examples of many nationalities' specialties: spinning, weaving, cabinetry, pottery, basketry, and metalwork. Addams also began musical evenings, where voices in a multitude of languages were raised in song. She was learning that America's much-vaunted "cultural superiority" might be a myth.

In the 10 years that followed the establishment of Hull House, the settlement movement had begun to spread across the United States. By 1891, six settlement houses had opened; nine years later, more than a hundred were in operation. In 1892, the School of Applied Ethics in Plymouth, Massachusetts, invited an imposing array of clergymen, economists, and sociologists to a conference on social progress and settlements. Among the participants was Jane Addams of Hull House.

Thanks to her many speeches and her numerous and prominent local supporters, Addams had become something of a celebrity in Chicago. Reports of her work at Hull House had also been studied with interest by other social workers across the nation. When she arrived at the 1892 conference, she found herself—somewhat to her surprise—considered the leader of the settlement-house movement. She gave two lectures at Plymouth, explaining why she thought settlement houses were essential and describing the activities of Hull House. During the discussions that followed, she was surrounded by the other eminent panelists, all of them eager to hear more of her ideas.

A Hull House neighbor spins thread at the settlement-house museum. Addams believed such demonstrations would increase ethnic pride among younger immigrants.

Addams's speeches at the Plymouth conference were reprinted, first in the widely read *Forum* magazine and then as part of a book, *Philanthropy and Social Progress*. The following year, 1893, she presided over another conference, this one held in Chicago and attended by settlement workers from Boston, Chicago, and New York City. Next, she made a tour of settlement houses in Massachusetts, New York, and Pennsylvania.

Everywhere she went, Addams was received as a pioneer, honored for her work in awakening the social con-

science of America. She even acquired an informal new title, half-affectionate, half-respectful: "Lady Jane." Writing to her sister from Philadelphia, the 33-year-old social worker said with amusement, "I find I am considered quite the grandmother of American settlements."

Hull House was becoming famous, a symbol of the new wave of altruism (unselfish concern for others) that was sweeping through the current generation of young, middle-class Americans. The Chicago settlement house, always crowded with neighborhood residents, became a magnet for visitors from all walks of life.

One journalist called Hull House "Jane Addams's salon of democracy." Through its doors, he said, "there passes a procession of Greek fruit vendors, university professors, mayors, aldermen, club-women, factory inspectors, novelists, reporters, policemen, Italian washerwomen, socialists, big businessmen, English members of Parliament, German scientists, and all other sorts and conditions of men."

After spending several months in 1893 studying Chicago's slums, British editor and journalist William Stead wrote *If Christ Came to Chicago*, a best-selling book about conditions among the city's poor. "If Christ came to Chicago," asked Stead, "what would he discover? Vice, criminality, corruption, and above all, neglect such as no other late 19th-century city would tol-

Carrying their night's work, a garment-factory worker and her son head for their daytime jobs. Addams crusaded for laws to protect working women and children.

William Stead, the British author of If Christ Came to Chicago, *was horrified by the city's slums but deeply impressed by the work Addams was doing there.*

erate." Stead then asserted that the "best hope for Chicago is the multiplication of Hull House into all the slum districts of the city."

Despite her steadily increasing fame, Addams continued the day-to-day work she had always done. In 1892, she directed a committee of Hull House staff members to make a thorough study of Chicago's garment industry, which employed thousands of children. She had always been deeply disturbed by the exploitation of children as menial laborers. As late as the 1890s there were no laws regulating

child labor. Employers were free to hire anyone of any age, and there were no limits on the number of hours a child could work. The Hull House committee's report was written in careful, unemotional prose, but the facts it revealed about child-labor conditions were shocking.

It noted that, like countless other very young Americans, thousands of Chicago youngsters worked factory shifts of 12 to 14 hours a day, 6 days a week. The smallest children were hired because they could scramble amid dangerous machinery or even

A spinning-machine operator gazes wistfully from a factory window. Until the early 1900s, America's workforce included children as young as five.

climb onto it—while it was running—to adjust it. Injuries among the child laborers, many times caused by a lack of elementary safety precautions, were frequent and often fatal. After work, the factory children brought their wages home to add to their families' meager resources. Too tired to play, they lived the harshest kind of adult life before they even reached their teenage years.

Publication of the Hull House child-labor report resulted in passage of the Illinois Factory Act of 1893, one of America's earliest attempts to regulate the hours and conditions of child labor. The legislation, said crusading journalist Henry D. Lloyd, was "the best anti-sweatshop law on the statute books of any civilized community."

Chicago's 19th Ward, where Hull House was situated, was among the filthiest in a city universally regarded as one of the worst-kept in the nation. Addams's desire to clean up the neighborhood had so far taken second place to more urgent business, but in 1894, it became a personal priority.

Her sister Mary had just died after a long illness, and Addams had been appointed guardian of her nephew (and future biographer), James Linn. She had planned to bring the boy to live with her at Hull House, but his doctor vetoed the plan. James did not have a very strong constitution, said the medical man; living in the foul and disease-ridden 19th Ward might en-danger his health, even kill him. James was sent away to school.

Addams later wrote that she was "ashamed" she had not acted earlier. The example of other children, "torn from their families, not into boarding-school but into eternity," should, she felt, have driven her into effective ac-tion long before. She vowed to turn her formidable energy toward the garbage-strewn streets of the 19th Ward.

James Linn later described the scene that inspired her commitment. "The streets were covered inches deep with packed and dirty refuse over broken pavements; the miry alleys smelled like sewers, and the sewers themselves were in hundreds of cases unconnect-ed with the houses; the stables, of which there were many, were inex-pressibly foul; courtyards [were] thick with babies and vermin."

Street corners in the 19th Ward fea-tured huge wooden garbage boxes in which, as Addams noted, "the undis-turbed refuse accumulated day by day." When the boxes were filled, gar-bage overflowed onto the streets and sidewalks, making walking a danger-ous adventure at best. Addams de-cided to attack this problem first in her campaign to clean up the streets.

The city of Chicago paid indepen-dent contractors to remove trash, but the city's administration was notori-ously corrupt; bribes placed in the proper official's hands enabled con-

Boys stoke the furnaces in a glass factory in 1905. At this time, American child laborers received an average wage of 40 cents per 12-hour day.

tractors to do no work and still collect their money. Addams and her assistants prowled the streets, noting violations of the sanitation laws and reporting them to the health department, but nothing changed. Finally, "in sheer desperation," Addams herself applied for the job of garbage contractor.

Her application was rejected, but it had set off a wave of citywide publicity. Embarrassed city officials hastily gave her the job of "ward garbage inspector" at a salary of $1,000 per year. This

position, the only salaried one Addams would ever hold, started a new uproar. Politicians who disliked Addams's "meddling" in city affairs accused her of accepting a sinecure (a paid job requiring no work). She defended herself vigorously.

"The position," she said, was "no sinecure." She pointed out that it involved reporting for work at six in the morning to make sure the collection crews were working and then following their reeking wagons to the city dump. (Without constant supervision, she discovered, the crews would simply unload the refuse a few blocks from where they picked it up.)

The 19th Ward began to lose its familiar odor, but local politicians remained unhappy. Eventually, they managed to pass a new city ruling that eliminated the job of garbage inspector altogether; the work would be done by a ward superintendent—a job open only to men.

Addams had lost the job but won her point, and she was pleased. The improved sanitation measures, she wrote, "brought about a great improvement in the cleanliness and comfort of the neighborhood." Even better was the improvement in residents' health. The piles of rotting garbage, which had attracted disease-carrying flies and other insects, were gone. After the cleanup, Addams reported, "the death rate of our ward was found to have dropped from third to seventh in the list of city wards." The news, she said, made "one happy day" for Hull House and its neighbors.

Although Addams's tenure as ward garbage inspector was not long, it made her more nationally famous than anything she had yet done at Hull House. "The image of the brave . . .

Young chimney sweeps display their tools in 1890. Such workers faced backbreaking labor, long hours, low pay, and highly dangerous working conditions.

woman battling the establishment and following the garbage carts to make her neighborhood safer and cleaner," observed biographer Allen Davis, "established her reputation as a practical and determined reformer." But Jane Addams had only begun to fight.

By 1899—10 years after she had opened Hull House—the 39-year-old Addams had become America's best-known champion of the poor and oppressed.

SIX

"A Big Woman"

Jane Addams had grown up in a prosperous family; she had traveled in luxury and had never lacked food, clothing, or material comforts. Not until she moved to Hull House had she ever come into close contact with the poor, with working men and women, with immigrants, with children who labored. But she quickly learned to understand her new neighbors.

After her firsthand introduction to Chicago's teeming 19th Ward, she became an impassioned protector of the oppressed and exploited. She was to become one of America's principal defenders of the social and economic group that is known today as the "underclass."

Extremely sympathetic to the people who labored long hours for low wages, Addams thought they had every right to organize themselves into unions.

She believed that labor unions should work toward harmony, relying on peaceful persuasion to achieve their goals. She firmly opposed strikes because they so often led to violence.

In the late 19th century, a deep division existed between America's upper and lower classes. Most prosperous people regarded the working class with suspicion and unions with outright hostility. Because Addams permitted several unions to hold meetings at Hull House, often invited labor leaders to visit the settlement, and frequently spoke out on behalf of the rights of the working class, she was regarded by many conservatives as a socialist, or worse, an anarchist.

Socialism, a political and economic doctrine based in part on a belief in public ownership of property, was considered dangerous by most of the

A bomb explodes during the Haymarket Riot, triggered by a police attack on an 1886 Chicago labor rally. Four alleged anarchists were hanged after the riot.

upper and middle class, but anarchism was viewed with downright horror. Its basic goal was universal justice, which its adherents believed could be achieved only after the elimination of all forms of government. There were, in fact, very few committed anarchists in the United States, but the popular imagination saw the movement as a serious threat to everything worthwhile in America.

European immigration increased dramatically in the 1880s. In 1882 alone, for example, 789,000 newcomers were admitted to the United States. Many Americans, who considered socialism and anarchism "foreign ideas," wrongly believed that they "infected" the entire immigrant population. The majority of America's immigrants were neither socialists nor anarchists. Like them, Jane Addams espoused neither doctrine, but after 1894 a large number of her fellow citizens would accuse her of being both—or worse.

In May 1894, workers at the Pullman Palace Car Company went on strike when the company management refused to discuss labor's grievances. The strike at Pullman, a Chicago factory that manufactured railroad cars, triggered a major work stoppage by the American Railway Union, paralyzing the rail system throughout the West. When thousands of nonunion workers, called "scabs" by the embattled union men, were imported from Canada to operate the railroads, violence was inevitable. Newspapers across the nation soon reported bloody clashes between regular workers and strikebreakers, destruction of railroad property, the arrest of union officials, and, finally, the arrival in Chicago of state and federal troops.

In an effort to restore peace at Pullman and to end the rail strike, the Civic Federation of Chicago appointed a six-person committee to negotiate with both sides. One member of the committee was Jane Addams. When Pullman company officials refused to

Self-described anarchist Leon Czolgosz peers from his cell after shooting President William McKinley in 1901. The crime increased Americans' fear of anarchism.

meet with the committee, Addams visited the factory herself. She told its managers that she believed some of the strikers' demands were justified; the managers told her to mind her own business.

Addams was not totally committed to the union point of view; she believed both sides had legitimate arguments. Her approach, in fact, was so evenhanded that it exasperated passionate labor supporters, one of whom was her old friend Ellen Starr. "If the devil

Soldiers fire at workers during the Pullman strike of 1894. Addams's efforts to be impartial in the labor dispute brought criticism from both sides.

himself came riding down Halsted Street with his tail waving out behind him," Starr told Addams, "you'd say, 'What a beautiful curve he has in his tail'!"

Addams believed labor and management had to learn to work together, each side gaining and conceding some of its demands. Hoping to make the Pullman strike issue clear to the public, she made speeches about it in several cities, including Chicago and Boston. She also wrote an article explaining her views.

Although the nation's leading magazines—*The Forum*, the *North American Review*, the *Century*, and the *Atlantic Monthly* among them—had eagerly published Addams's work in the past, none of them would run her piece about the strike. The editor of the *Atlantic Monthly* probably spoke for his colleagues when he explained that he could not in good conscience print an article implying that "Pullman was in the wrong."

Harrassed by both business and government and lacking funds to support a long strike, the unions finally gave up. Both Pullman and railway workers went back to work in midsummer on the same terms they had rejected earlier. Addams continued to speak out for fairness in the settlement of labor disputes. Although she criticized both sides in most worker-management disputes, her fundamental sympathy was with the workers.

After the Pullman strike, Addams hired only union labor for Hull House construction projects, and she demanded that her books be printed in union shops. When 40,000 Chicago textile workers struck for decent wages and working conditions, she collected money to help support their families. Because she was now a prominent figure, her actions and views attracted widespread attention—and widespread criticism. She was, said some, a "traitor to her class." She was also called other names, very few of them complimentary.

One important Chicago businessman said, "Jane Addams is no longer a safe leader to follow, she is becoming too socialistic in her tendencies." A Chicago newspaper ran an editorial asserting that Addams "should have said emphatically that violence practiced by the labor unions has made them infamous and that none of them should meet again at Hull House." A wealthy Chicagoan who had previously contributed to Hull House declined to continue his support. The settlement house, he said, "has become so thoroughly unionized that it has lost its usefulness and has become a detriment and harm to the community as a whole."

Addams was hurt by the negative remarks, but she continued to pursue the path she considered the right one. A fierce defender of the right of every American to freedom of speech, she welcomed the discussion of all points of view at Hull House, even if the speaker was an atheist or an anarchist. It was, she said impatiently, absurd to assume that "he who knows intimately people among whom anarchists arise is therefore an anarchist."

Criticized by some for being prolabor, Addams was attacked by others as promanagement. Nevertheless, her advice would continue to be sought by both sides in labor disputes. She would serve on arbitration committees during Chicago's major building-trade strike in 1900, the national coal-miners' strike of 1902, the Chicago stockyards strike in 1904, and a massive textile-workers' strike in 1910, among others. The tex-

tile strike ended typically: Addams had been instrumental in bringing the strikers and the mill owners together, but when they set up a permanent arbitration board, it did not include her; each side believed she favored the other.

Hull House remained the center of Addams's life in the 1890s and the first decade of the 20th century, but she did not limit her activities to Chicago. With seemingly inexhaustible energy, she made speeches all over the United States. In February 1899, for example, she delivered 4 lectures in New York

An Italian family arrives at New York City's Ellis Island. Between 1881 and 1900, almost 9 million immigrants settled in the United States.

State, 10 in Massachusetts, 2 in Pennsylvania, and 1 each in Vermont, Virginia, and South Carolina. The more often she spoke, the more confident she became. In the middle of a 1902 lecture tour, she wrote to a friend, "I will confide in you alone that I have never spoken so well and so many times as during this trip. It has altogether been successful.... I expect to go home prepared for valiant deeds."

During the rare moments when she was not supervising the programs at Hull House, taking part in labor-management meetings, or making speeches, Addams wrote her first book. Published in 1902, *Democracy and Social Ethics* was a resounding success. Harvard College's eminent philosopher-psychologist, William James, called it "one of the great books of our time." U.S. Supreme Court Justice Oliver Wendell Holmes said Addams was "a big woman." She "gives me," he added, "more insights into the point of view of the working man and the poor than I had before." Another reviewer—obviously a man—praised Addams's work in his own way. "No other book by a woman," he asserted, "shows such vitality, such masculinity of mental grasp."

Democracy and Social Ethics was a study of the relationships among human beings. It also dealt sympathetically with America's immigrants and their difficulties in exchanging familiar languages and social customs for the

Women textile workers picket in 1910. Addams, as usual, saw both sides in the huge strike; in the end, neither labor nor management trusted her.

alien practices of a new world. Addams's concern about minority groups included blacks, whom she saw facing many of the same problems as immigrants. Slavery, which had ended in the United States only a few decades earlier, had both broken up black families and deprived them of contact with their cultural heritage.

Few blacks lived near Hull House, but Addams helped found Wendell Phillips Settlement, a community project serving black residents in a nearby, racially mixed neighborhood. She attended meetings of the National Association of Colored Women and frequently invited eminent black leaders, including educator Booker T. Washington, to Hull House. When she addressed the National Convention of

Women's Clubs in Los Angeles in 1902, she startled many conservative representatives by proposing that black women's organizations be offered membership in the association. When the National Association for the Advancement of Colored People was organized in 1909, Addams was a member of its executive committee.

In an era when many whites looked the other way in cases of lynching—the hunting down and killing of blacks suspected of crimes against whites—Addams spoke out forcefully. Lynch victims were often black men who had been falsely accused of raping white women. Addams was particularly outraged by those who saw such murders as a legitimate defense of "white womanhood." In one typical antilynching speech, she condemned the idea that justice could be bought at the price of "human blood and the burning of human flesh."

"To those who say that most of these hideous and terrorizing acts have been committed in . . . order to make the lives and honor of [white] women safe," she said, "perhaps it is women themselves who can best . . . testify that the honor of women is only secure in those nations and those localities where law and order and justice prevail."

Occasionally Addams had to struggle to live by convictions that often seemed to collide. At one point, she hired a black cook for Hull House. She made it a practice to employ only union labor, but Chicago's food-trades unions accepted only white members. Addams solved the dilemma in a characteristically practical way: She arranged for the new cook to join a racially mixed St. Louis union and continued to champion both racial equality and the rights of organized labor.

Addams's concern for humanity took many forms, but her desire to

Educator Booker T. Washington was one of many black leaders who visited Addams at Hull House. Born a slave in 1856, Washington wrote Up From Slavery *in 1901.*

A lynch mob attacks a defenseless black man in 1882. Addams, who often spoke out for black victims of oppression, denounced lynching as a "hideous act."

help eliminate poverty remained central. She read everything she could find about other movements, both in the United States and abroad, that aimed at helping the poor. She was especially interested in the writings of Russian novelist and philosopher Leo Tolstoy. The author of such masterpieces as *War and Peace* and *Anna Karenina*, Tolstoy had abandoned his luxurious life-style to live among the impoverished peasants of his native land. In 1896, Addams went to visit the celebrated Russian at his home, which was east of Moscow, the Russian capital.

Tolstoy, who was then almost 70 years old, was a wealthy man. Nevertheless, he worked in the fields along-side his peasant neighbors, wore the same rough clothing, and ate the same simple food. He was interested in Addams's description of Hull House and its neighbors, but puzzled by her fashionable clothes.

"Tolstoy standing by clad in his peasant garb listened gravely," she recalled later, "but, glancing at the sleeves of my traveling gown which unfortunately at that season were monstrous in size, he...said that there was enough stuff in one arm to make a frock [dress] for a little girl." Did she, he asked gently, "not find such a dress a barrier to the people?" Addams was, she remembered, "disconcerted" by the great man's questions, but she managed to explain that "the working girls in Chicago" wore similar clothing, and "that nothing could more effectively separate" her from them than the wearing of self-consciously "simple" clothing.

That point answered, the Russian author and the American social worker went on to discuss many things, among them "social democracy" and Tolstoy's ideas about "Christian anarchy" and nonviolence. Addams was deeply impressed by Tolstoy, whom she called "one of the gentlest and kindest of human creatures I ever saw." She was particularly intrigued by the Russian's insistence that, without international peace, the lot of mankind could not be improved. Tolstoy's concept of pacifism would have a strong effect on Jane Addams, leading her to new glory—and making her, for a time, one of the most detested women in America.

Russian novelist and moral philosopher Leo Tolstoy, a wealthy aristocrat, chose to spend his later years living among the poor. Addams visited him in 1896.

Addams remained committed to Hull House throughout her life, but after the Spanish-American War in 1898, she spent more and more time working for world peace.

SEVEN

From "Bull Moose" to "Bull Mouse"

Until she discussed pacifism with Leo Tolstoy in 1896, Jane Addams had given little thought to international affairs. Even after she had talked to the Russian writer, such issues had more philosophic than practical interest for her. Her immediate concerns had always been specific: the well-being of her neighbors, the security of their jobs and homes, the problems of immigrants and blacks, the rights of workers to unionize. Her attitude toward war and peace, however, began to change at the end of the Spanish-American War, the short 1898 conflict in which the United States acquired the Philippines, Puerto Rico, and, temporarily, Cuba.

Characteristically, Addams's interest in the war was piqued by its effect on the area in which she lived and worked, Chicago's 19th Ward. Watch-ing the local children as they "played war" in the streets, she observed that they were not "freeing Cubans," but "slaying Spaniards." It suddenly occurred to her that the children's attitude reflected a dangerous shift in the attitude of American society as a whole. "The spectacle of war," she declared in an 1898 speech, "has been a great setback to the development and growth of the higher impulse of civilization."

Addams's reaction to the children's games was to have far-reaching effects on her life. She was, as biographer Allen Davis put it, "taking the first halting steps toward formulating a theory for a substitute for the war spirit"— for what she could later call "a moral equivalent for war." In an 1899 speech about war, she said: "Let us not glorify the brutality. The same strenuous en-

Sunk by an explosion, the U.S. battleship Maine *lies off Havana, Cuba, in 1898. The ship's destruction, blamed on Spain, started the Spanish-American War.*

deavor, the same heroic self-sacrifice, the same fine courage and readiness to meet death may be displayed without the accompaniment of killing our fellow men."

The Spanish-American War left Americans with a glow of satisfaction in their nation's military strength, a mood Addams regarded as ominous. "We allure our young men not to develop but to exploit," she said in a speech in 1900. "We incite their ambitions not to irrigate, to make fertile . . .

the barren plain of the savage, but to fill it with military posts." In 1901, when British forces fought the South Africans during the Boer War, she went further in her denunciation of military conflict. "War in all its horror is a terrible thing," she said. "It is the law of the jungle elaborated."

In 1903 she began a new book, this one offering her thoughts on "dynamic peace." Finally published in 1907 as *Newer Ideals of Peace*, it received mixed reactions. Theodore Roosevelt, hero of the Spanish-American War and 26th president of the United States, was among the book's harshest critics. Labeling it "sentimental" and "naive," the president said "foolish Jane Addams" lacked the "strength, training, and natural ability" to deal with issues of peace and war. Others, however, had high praise for Addams's book. The Chicago *Evening Post*, for example, called it a "profound and searching, as well as practical, analysis of American tendencies."

The writing of a long, serious book might have been a full-time occupation for some people but not for Addams; while she worked on the book, she juggled her usual variety of projects. Many of them were connected with the young people whom she had always welcomed at Hull House.

As James Linn noted in his Addams biography, "If a little girl was beaten by her drunken father, she came crying to Hull House to tell Miss Addams; if a

Spanish-American War hero Theodore Roosevelt (center) stands proudly with his troops. A staunch militarist, he detested Addams's book Newer Ideals of Peace.

boy playing in the court broke a Hull House window, he did not run away but stayed where he was, confident that Miss Addams would 'fix it.' Girls who had been arrested for picketing, girls who were in love, girls who were 'in trouble,' girls who had been caught in raids by the police, girls who had no 'right dress' to be married in, girls who were 'afraid they were going crazy,' came to see her. . . . She shrank from no young thing, no matter what it had been or done."

Addams had long worried about Chicago's treatment of juvenile offenders, who were tried in regular courts and, if convicted, jailed with adult criminals. She and her associates cam-

paigned long and hard for a special court where young people accused of breaking the law could be tried separately. The efforts of the Hull House team resulted in the establishment of Chicago's Juvenile Court, the first in the nation.

Their efforts also resulted in Addams's next book, *The Spirit of Youth and the City Streets*, published in 1909. Among the subjects the book covered was juvenile delinquency. Addams disputed the popular theory that criminality was an inherited trait; juvenile delinquents, she maintained, were produced by the environment in which they grew up. *The Spirit of Youth*—Addams's personal favorite

Woman-suffrage workers campaign in New York harbor in 1914, six years before women got the vote. Addams had been an active suffragist since 1897.

among her books—was praised by sociologists, politicians, and general readers.

The following year, 1910, Addams published her autobiography, *Twenty Years at Hull House*, which became an instant best seller. The Portland *Evening Telegram* called it "a book which breathes on every page the spirit of a dedicated life." The Baltimore *Sun* said it was "the most important book of the year." Translated versions of *Twenty Years at Hull House* appeared in Germany, France, and Japan, where Addams acquired legions of new admirers. One German reader wrote to Addams, "You have enlarged the word

'American' for me." Still in print more than 75 years later, Addams's autobiography continues to sell briskly.

Addams followed up *Twenty Years* with *A New Conscience and an Ancient Evil*, a study of prostitution in America. Although a few critics disliked the book (one called it "hysterical"), most treated it as a modern masterpiece. Addams's pen, said a typical reviewer, was "dipped in sincerity, truth and wisdom." By now, Jane Addams was one of the best-known women in the United States. Social worker, reformer, spokesperson for the oppressed, she was seen by millions of Americans as the embodiment of "female virtue," a crusader who represented the finest part of the nation's character. It was at this point that she entered national politics.

The 1912 presidential race was unusual. Theodore Roosevelt, who had served as president from 1901 to 1909, had decided to run for the office again. Unable to secure the Republican nomination, he had "bolted" and formed his own political organization, the Progressive, or "Bull Moose," party. Thus, three candidates vied for the presidency: Democrat Woodrow Wilson, Republican William H. Taft, and Progressive Theodore Roosevelt.

Before the 1912 election, the National Conference of Charities and Correction, a coalition of social workers headed by Jane Addams, presented a list of its goals to the Republican party.

The coalition's demands included an eight-hour work day, a six-day work week, the prohibition of child labor, and a federal system of old-age, accident, and unemployment insurance.

Taft and the Republicans showed no interest in these measures, but Roosevelt and his Progressives did. The newly formed party did more than adopt the social workers' program; it announced its support of woman suffrage, or women's right to vote. Although Jane Addams had not been among the pioneer suffragists, she had advocated voting rights for women since 1897. She had joined the National American Woman Suffrage Association in 1906 and become its vice-president in 1911.

When Roosevelt endorsed both labor reform and votes for women, Addams forgot his earlier sharp criticism of her work. Abandoning her lifelong political neutrality, she made a public announcement: "The Progressive platform," she said, "contains all the things I have been fighting for for more than a decade."

Roosevelt was officially nominated for the presidency at the Progressive party convention, held in Chicago in August 1912. His nomination was seconded by Jane Addams. "A great party has pledged itself to the protection of children, to the care of the aged, to the relief of overworked girls, to the safeguarding of burdened men," she said. "Roosevelt," she continued, "is one of the few men in our public life who has been responsive to the social appeal and who has caught the significance of the modern movement."

Addams saw the election less as a political mission than as a crusade for social justice and women's rights. She campaigned vigorously, writing articles for newspapers and magazines and making speeches from Massachusetts to Oklahoma, from Nebraska to Missouri. Everywhere she went she was greeted by huge crowds of cheering people, their enthusiasm sparked as much by Addams as by the candidate she endorsed. One party worker observed, "Wherever I went I heard nothing but talk of Jane Addams. I suppose other political speakers had been out there, but you never would have guessed it from what people had to say."

Despite Roosevelt's personal magnetism and Addams's enormous popularity, the Progressive party lost; Woodrow Wilson became the nation's 28th president. Roosevelt's defeat neither surprised nor depressed Addams. She felt that her time and that of the other Progressives had been well spent in calling the public's attention to important causes.

"I had expected from the beginning that Mr. Wilson was to be the next president," she told a newspaper reporter. But, she added, "the principles enunciated in the Progressive platform afforded the opportunity for giving

French troops attack Germans with flamethrowers during World War I. Shocked by the war's death toll, Addams urged the U.S. government to act as peacemaker.

wide publicity to the necessity for social and industrial reforms." Theodore Roosevelt would never again be a major political force, but Addams's reputation had been enhanced. She was now famous not only in her own country but around the world, admired and respected for her convictions and her actions.

Because newspaper editors knew the public wanted to read stories about Addams, they often reported on her. Readers always knew who was meant by such titles as "The Only American Saint," "The Genius of Hull House," "Chicago's First Citizen," and "The First Lady of the Land." One public-opinion poll named Addams "the best woman in Chicago," and another put her at the top of the list of the "25 greatest women in history." In 1913, when 3,000 representative citizens were asked to list the "12 most socially useful Americans," Addams again topped the list, ahead of Theodore Roosevelt and Thomas Edison.

Within a year, however, Addams's extraordinary popularity with her fellow citizens would vanish. Almost overnight, she was publicly demoted from "first lady of the land" to "silly, vain, impertinent old maid." The story of this astonishing transformation began with the outbreak of war in Europe in 1914.

Divided by a complex set of alliances, the major nations of Europe had long been tense, suspicious of one another, and ready to mobilize their armies. On June 28, 1914, Archduke Francis Ferdinand of Austria-Hungary was assassinated by a Serbian terrorist. The murder sparked an international explosion; in a matter of weeks, all the major countries of Europe were at war. World War I, as the conflict came to be called, aligned Germany, Austria-Hungary, and Turkey (the Central Powers) against Britain, France, and Russia (the Allies).

Like most Americans, Jane Addams was horrified to hear of the "wholesale slaughter of thousands of men a day" in Europe. Sentiment in the United States, however, was not unanimous about what course of action the nation should follow. Many Americans, seeing the European conflict as a direct threat to their homeland, favored an immediate military buildup. Others, Addams included, thought the role of the United States should be that of peacemaker, working through diplomacy to bring a speedy end to the war.

Soon after the war began, Addams became the leader of the Emergency Federation of Peace Forces, an umbrella association of antiwar organizations. The group hoped to pressure the American government into forming

The Lusitania *leaves New York harbor in 1915. Germany sank the British liner a week later, killing 128 Americans and bringing the United States closer to war.*

a league of neutral nations that could bring the war to a halt. Realizing they would need widespread support from other groups to achieve this, Addams and her associates called a meeting of American women's organizations in Washington, D.C.

On January 10, 1915, 3,000 women gathered in the nation's capital to plan their strategy. It was an all-star event. Attending were many of the most prominent women in the country: writers, lecturers, college professors, sociologists, and representatives of such groups as the American School Peace League, the American Peace Society, and the Anti-Imperialist League.

U.S. automobile tycoon Henry Ford (with bowler hat) embarks on a private peace mission to Europe. Ridiculed by all sides, the 1915 trip accomplished nothing.

The women's coalition drafted a program calling for a convention of neutral nations to stop the war. The manifesto opened with a statement that read in part: "We, women of the United States, assembled in behalf of world peace, grateful for the security of our own country but sorrowing for the misery of all involved in the present struggle among warring nations, do hereby ... demand that war be abolished.... So demanding, we hereby form ourselves into a national organization to be called the Woman's Peace Party."

There was no debate about who should lead the new party; chosen of course, was Jane Addams. The following April, she led a group of Woman's Peace Party delegates to the Netherlands (one of the few neutral European countries), where they took part in an international conference of women dedicated to ending the war. The delegates hammered out a series of peace demands addressed to the leaders of both warring and neutral nations. Addams was elected to deliver the message to the belligerents.

She doubted that such a pilgrimage would change the course of the war, but she was, she told a friend, "willing to do anything" to help obtain peace. With three other conference delegates, she visited seven nations, including Britain, Germany, and Austria. The group received a chilly reception everywhere but Vienna. Austria's prime minister was silent as Addams outlined the Peace Party's proposals. "It perhaps seems to you very foolish," she recalled saying to him, "that women should go about in this way...." To her astonishment, the prime minister slammed his hand on his desk.

"Foolish?" he thundered. "Not at all! These are the first sensible words that have been uttered in this room in 10 months!" His words, she said, made her mission "seem worthwhile," but, as she had feared, the trip accomplished little in the long run. The government leaders she had met, she told a reporter, "sympathized with the idea of bringing about a speedy peace" but committed themselves only to achieving victory for their own nations.

Few Americans had much hope for the success of Addams's peace mission, but many admired her for making the effort. As one newspaper editorial said, she and her associates "may not have succeeded in restoring peace, but they will at least have given voice to the humane instincts of the world." Another editorial asked, "Who shall make bold to call [the women's trip] a failure? Who can deny that they have sown seeds of conciliation that may take root even in hearts now stony, and bear fruit in time?"

Making a speech in New York City soon after her return to the United States, Addams said she had found the people of Europe brave and patriotic, working hard for their own nation's well-deserved victory. However, she added, she was sure that few Europeans wanted war. They had no wish to kill, no eagerness to send sons and husbands to death on the battlefield. She told of meeting a young soldier who said that "nothing in the world could make him kill another man." She told of soldiers about to go to the front lines who committed suicide, "not because they were afraid of being killed, but because they were afraid ... they would have to kill someone else."

Addams (center) and other Woman's Peace Party delegates arrive in the Netherlands in 1915. The Americans were in Europe for an antiwar conference.

A French rifleman fires over a fallen comrade. Americans were enraged when Addams said that soldiers' courage often came from liquor received before battles.

Then she spoke the words that shattered her reputation. All the warring nations, she said, had discovered "the necessity for the use of stimulant before men would engage in bayonet charges—that they have a regular formula in Germany, that they give them rum in England and absinthe in France; that they have to give them the 'dope' before the bayonet charge is possible."

Addams had the deepest respect and sympathy for the young soldiers who were fighting and dying in Europe. But what she said was true; many armies distributed wine or whiskey to soldiers to raise their spirits before battle. She had mentioned it to

demonstrate the ugliness of war, which many of her fellow citizens still regarded as exciting and romantic.

She had, however, struck a nerve. Her words were widely interpreted to mean that *all* soldiers were cowards who had to be gotten drunk before they would fight. Americans, who cherished the image of the gallant soldier laying down his life for his country, were outraged by Addams's observations. The next day, her speech was front-page news across the country. TROOPS DRINK-CRAZED, SAYS MISS ADDAMS, screamed one newspaper headline.

The first salvo against Addams was fired by celebrated writer and war correspondent Richard Harding Davis. "Miss Addams," he wrote in the *New York Times*, "denies [the soldier] the credit of his sacrifice. She strips him of honor and courage. She tells his children, 'Your father did not die for France, or for England, or for you; he died because he was drunk.' . . . Against this insult, flung by a complacent and self-satisfied woman at men who gave their lives for men, I protest."

The assaults grew fiercer. One newspaper called Addams "a silly, vain, impertinent old maid, who may have done good charity work at Hull House, Chicago, but is now meddling in affairs far beyond her capacity." Another said, "The time was when Miss Jane Addams . . . held a warm place in the hearts of the American people but she

Richard Harding Davis attacked Addams for mentioning government-issued "stimulants" for soldiers. Her words, said the famed war reporter, were an "insult."

Addams, vilified for her views on war, refused to despair. Quoting her friend Booker T. Washington, she said, "I will permit no man to make me hate him!"

is fast losing [their] esteem." The Louisville *Courier* called her "a foolish, garrulous [overtalkative] woman."

Addams was attacked not only in newspapers and magazines but in speeches by prominent Americans. One of them was Theodore Roosevelt. After referring to his former political ally as "poor bleeding Jane," and calling her a member of "the shrieking sisterhood," the old Bull Moose delivered the ultimate insult. Addams, he said scornfully, had turned into a "Bull Mouse."

The beleaguered social worker also received mountains of personal mail. A few people wrote to congratulate her for speaking out, but most of the letters were abusive. One newspaper editor summed up the situation: "If Jane Addams is a careful reader of the newspapers, she must have discovered by this time that any popular idol can be knocked from its pedestal by talking too much."

Although she was distressed by the wave of criticism, Addams was not defeated. "It was at this time," she wrote later, "that I first learned to use for my own edification a statement of Booker Washington's: 'I will permit no man to make me hate him!'" Neither would she permit anyone—then or ever—to keep her from "talking too much" about what she believed to be true.

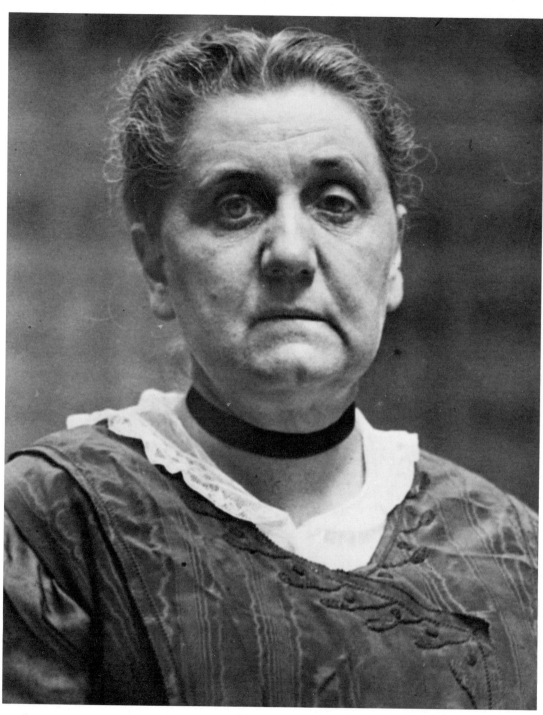

By the mid-1920s, many Americans despised the once-beloved Addams. Her passionate, outspoken defense of unpopular views had made her an outcast.

EIGHT

"America's Most Dangerous Woman"

In August 1914, soon after war broke out in Europe, American president Woodrow Wilson had sent a message to Congress: "The United States must be neutral in fact as well as in name," he said. "We must be impartial in thought as well as action." Two and one-half years later, in April 1917, Wilson told Congress that "neutrality is no longer feasible or desirable." Responding to the president's request, Congress voted overwhelmingly to go to war. The United States joined England and France in their battle against Germany and the Central Powers.

Wilson had sincerely wanted to keep the nation out of the war, but the appeals of the Allies, coupled with the sinking of several American ships by German submarines, had made continued neutrality impossible. Popular sentiment in the United States was another factor: Outraged by the German attacks, the public had clamored for war.

A small but determined minority of Americans, which included Jane Addams, had firmly disapproved of America's entry into the "Great War," as the conflict was then known. Once it had become a reality, however, most Americans, even former peace activists, supported the war effort. Addams remained a staunch pacifist.

Instead of victory, she said, the United States should pursue a quick, negotiated peace, followed by "the creation of an international government." In a nation aflame with patriotism and hatred of the "Huns" (Germans), Addams's position was, not surprisingly, extremely unpopular.

Undaunted, she continued to speak out. "The pacifists of today," she said

President Woodrow Wilson asks Congress to declare war on Germany in 1917. America joined the Allies, but Addams remained an unshakable pacifist.

in a 1917 lecture in Evanston, Illinois, "urge upon the United States not isolation, not indifference to moral issues and to the fate of liberty and democracy." What they did want, she asserted, was "a strenuous endeavor to lead all nations of the earth into an organized international life worthy of civilized men."

When Addams finished speaking, a member of the audience stood up. An Illinois judge, he had been one of Hull House's early supporters. "I have always been a friend of Miss Addams," he began, "but . . ."

Addams gently interrupted him. "The 'but' sounds as if you were going to break with me," she said with a smile.

"I *am* going to break with you," shouted the judge. "Anything which tends to cast doubt on the justice of our cause in the present war is very unfortunate. No pacifist measures should be taken until the war is over!" With that speech, Addams's old friend stormed out of the lecture hall, leaving reporters busily scribbling down his words for the next day's newspapers.

Addams kept on "casting doubt," the papers kept reporting her views, and hate mail kept pouring in. One of the more restrained letters said, "My Dear Miss Addams, believe me, you are an awful ass, truly awful. . . . Each time you open your mouth nowadays and each time you write one of your unpatriotic and pro-German speeches you proclaim yourself an ass."

Addams, observed biographer Allen Davis, "had come full circle, from heroine, to high-minded fool, to villain. . . . Just as [she] was formerly praised and worshiped for her altruism by people who felt guilty about their own acquisitiveness, so now she could be denounced for her opposition to the war by people who felt ambivalence [uncertainty] and fear about the horrors of armed conflict, yet would not admit it."

Being cast as a villain was dispiriting, even for the usually buoyant Addams. She wrote later that she felt a sense of "widespread misunderstanding which brought me very near to self-pity, perhaps the lowest pit into which human nature can sink." She had discovered, she said, that an individual could "travel from the mire of self-pity straight to the barren hills of self-righteousness and to hate himself equally in both places."

Although she never wavered in her opposition to the war, Addams was feeling increasingly useless in a country where everyone else seemed to be working for the war effort. Then, early in 1918, she discovered a way to contribute to humanity without compromising her beliefs. She was offered a job by Food Administration director Herbert Hoover, the Iowa mining engineer who, in 1929, would become the nation's 31st president.

Hoover's wartime agency, responsible for civilian and military food pro-

A wartime poster asks Americans to conserve food. Addams's lectures on behalf of the Food Administration helped to brighten her tarnished image.

Be Patriotic
**sign your country's
pledge to save the food**

U.S. FOOD ADMINISTRATION

New Yorkers sing the national anthem during a patriotic rally in 1917. After war had been declared, most Americans supported it wholeheartedly.

duction and distribution, needed a well-known American to explain its mission to the public. Hoover told Addams she was the ideal candidate for the job, which would involve touring the United States and teaching women how to produce more food and how to conserve it. She accepted the post without hesitation.

Until the war ended with the victory of the Allies in November 1918, Addams crisscrossed the country, talking to women at schools, county fairs, and club meetings. She spoke not only about the best ways to raise and preserve food but about the role of women as "bread-givers" and family providers. No one had wanted to hear what she said about war and peace, but American women listened attentively when her subject was food.

Reporting on her lectures in California, the *Los Angeles Times* noted that she had been "blessed indeed" when she had "worked for the alleviation of sorrow," but that she had made a serious mistake: She had "stood forth for peace when there was no peace, and made public utterances ... that were better left unsaid." The *Times* story, however, concluded on a positive note. "Now she is seeing clearly again," it said, "and her service is with the country, and with the administration, with the Allies, wholehearted and wholesouled. . . . She obviously stands before the country now an earnest, though sad, adherent of the Allies' cause."

Addams had regained a large measure of public respect, but it was to be short-lived. She could not and would not reshape her conscience to fit currently popular sentiments. Defying her country's bitter hatred of the vanquished enemy, she appealed for help for starving German children after the war. And when a strange and frightening postwar phenomenon known as the "Red Scare" swept the United States, she expressed her outrage, once again surrounding herself with bitter controversy and criticism.

Following a 1919 international women's conference in Switzerland, Addams and several of her associates went to Germany. She was shocked by what she saw: "incredibly pathetic children," many of them seriously ill, all of them desperately hungry. At one children's shelter she saw hundreds of listless, feeble youngsters waiting for their midday meal, "one pint of thin meal soup, to which had been added a little dried vegetable." The children, Addams recalled sorrowfully, were like "a line of moving skeletons."

On her return to the United States, Addams embarked on a fund-raising campaign for these innocent victims of war. Unless help arrived soon, she said, an entire generation in Germany would be "doomed to early death or a handicapped life." She was sure that the generous impulses of Americans would inspire a wish "to relieve suffering, to give food to the hungry and to shelter the homeless." She was wrong.

Their wartime hatred of the "savage Hun" undiminished by victory, Americans greeted Addams's pleas for the starving children of Germany with undisguised hostility. When she spoke in Cleveland, Ohio, for example, she was accused of giving "the most violently pro-German speech ever delivered in an American city." The reaction in other cities was similar; over and over, she was heckled, shouted down, called "un-American" and a "traitor."

Addams's popularity would sink even lower during the "Red Scare," a wave of nearly hysterical fear of communism that was inspired by the 1917

The U.S. government bombarded the nation with anti-German propaganda during the war. This poster includes a typical portrait of "the savage Hun."

Russian Revolution. Encouraged by A. Mitchell Palmer, Woodrow Wilson's attorney general, Americans began to suspect anyone with a foreign accent, anyone who had opposed the war, anyone who did not appear to be a "red-blooded American" as a dangerous radical. Acting on Palmer's orders, policemen illegally arrested thousands of Americans, many of them immi-

World War I ended on November 11, 1918, but rage against the "Huns" continued. Many Americans believed that all Germans should be severely punished.

German children line up for soup in 1918. When Addams tried to collect food for Germany's hungry population, she was called "un-American" and a "traitor."

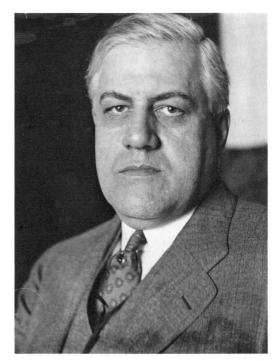

A. Mitchell Palmer, U.S. attorney general from 1919 to 1921, arrested thousands of innocent people as "radicals." Addams often spoke in defense of the accused.

grants, who were suspected of being "anarchists" or "reds."

Characteristically, Addams leapt to the defense of the imprisoned suspects. Addressing a 1920 meeting in Chicago, she said, "Hundreds of poor laboring men and women are being thrown into jails and police stations because of their political beliefs.... And what is it these radicals seek? It is the right of free speech and free thought; nothing more than is guaranteed to them under the Constitution of the United States.... Let us give these people a chance to explain their beliefs and desires. Let us end this supression and spirit of intolerance."

Although the speech was far from revolutionary, it was quoted as proof that Addams was dangerous. The next day's Chicago *Tribune* headlined its report, JANE ADDAMS FAVORS REDS. What followed was all too familiar. Addams was accused of spreading "insidious and mischievous propaganda," of using "perversion and distortion of the facts," of taking part in "pernicious, anti-American activities." One typical letter-writer offered his solution: "The radicals," he said, "are sworn enemies of our country and should be shot to death."

The 1920s are often remembered as the "Jazz Age." The decade was indeed noted for a kind of desperate gaiety: After the 18th Amendment outlawed liquor in 1920, "speakeasies" (illegal saloons) flourished and traditional rules of moral behavior were scrapped: Young men drank from hip flasks; young women bobbed their hair and shortened their skirts. It was an era of flashy roadsters, gang wars, "Charleston" dancing, and a new kind of entertainment: motion pictures. It was also the heyday of the radical right, when the public imagined that a gigantic communist conspiracy was preparing to destroy the United States.

As the mood of extreme political anxiety deepened, antipathy toward such "liberal" figures as Jane Addams intensified. The commander of the Illinois American Legion charged Hull House with being "the rallying point of every radical and communist movement in the country." The Daughters of the American Revolution (DAR) included Addams in a book called *The Common Enemy* and on a list of "doubtful speakers." *Scabbard and Blade*, an influential military publication, called her "the most dangerous woman in America."

A British physician who had long admired Addams summed up the social worker's position in the mid-1920s. "In America in 1912 I learned that it was unsafe to mention Jane Addams's name in public speech unless you were prepared for an interruption, because the mere reference to her provoked such a storm of applause," recalled the doctor. "And I was in America again after the war, and I realized with a shock how complete was the eclipse of her fame.... How well I remember, when I spoke in America in 1922 and 1923, the silence that greeted the name of Jane Addams! The few faithful who tried to applaud only made the silence more depressing."

Addams was not entirely without supporters. When the DAR announced that Addams was helping promote "a communist civil war in our country," even Carrie Chapman Catt rose to her defense. Catt, a prominent feminist who had disagreed with Addams on many issues, wrote an open letter to the DAR. "Miss Addams," said Catt, "is one of the greatest women this republic of ours has produced. She has given her life to serve others. She knows no selfish thought. You slap her on the right cheek; she only turns the left.... She is the kind of Christian who might have been thrown to the lions and would have gone cheerfully."

Addams did her best to behave "cheerfully." In a letter expressing her thanks to Catt, she said, "I have never taken these attacks very seriously, having learned during the war how ephemeral [fleeting] such matters are." Nevertheless, she was emotionally wounded by the constant assaults on her character. Aware of her pain, her friends often reminded her that the accusations came from America's "lunatic fringe," not the bulk of its people. This was true; also true, however, was the fact that such mudslinging deeply

Carrie Chapman Catt marches for woman suffrage in New York City. Catt frequently disagreed with Addams but vigorously defended her against charges of communism.

scarred Addams's reputation.

Still, she kept working. In 1922 she wrote *Peace and Bread in Time of War*, an explanation of her theories about pacifism and a discussion of women's role in keeping peace and nurturing humanity. The book was received quietly in the United States, but with great enthusiasm overseas, especially in England.

Rebuffed by many of her fellow Americans, Addams began to spend long periods abroad, working for the

Women's International League for Peace and Freedom. In Europe, India, the Philippines, China, and Japan she was greeted with respect and acclaim. Unlike many Americans, Europeans and Asians continued to regard her as a hero, a woman who represented the finest qualities of her nation.

From Japan, she wrote to a friend about the 5,000 schoolchildren who greeted her with flags and cheers: "I have never anywhere been so fêted [honored] as a peace advocate," she said. Although she claimed that the display was "positively embarrassing," it must have soothed her battered self-esteem.

Addams continued to manage Hull House, but because she spent so much time out of the country, much of her direction was long distance. She found her work with the Women's League both challenging and exhilarating. The league organized peace pilgrimages and demonstrations, investigated the opium trade, and sent delegations to the League of Nations and to the governments of the major world powers, urging that military conscription (the draft) be ended.

By the beginning of the 1930s, Americans had once again begun to see Addams as a figure worthy of respect. The passions aroused by World War I had faded with the years; furthermore, the threat of a new war in Europe made her pacifist views seem more reasonable. In 1931 she received an award for "eminent achievement" from Bryn Mawr College, the first of many institutions that would honor her in that decade.

Once again, her name appeared on the lists that Americans had long enjoyed compiling: She was named "the woman in her special field [who] has made the most distinguished contribution to American life"; she appeared on *Good Housekeeping* magazine's list of "America's Twelve Greatest Women"; her portrait was hung at Chicago's Century of Progress Exposition among those of the "Greatest American Women of the Century."

Colleges and universities, too, vied with each other in honoring Addams. In the 1930s, she received degrees from Northwestern University, the University of Chicago, Swarthmore College, the University of California, and Mount Holyoke College, among others. She had, in the words of biographer Allen Davis, "regained her position as both practical humanitarian and saint."

Accompanied by a fellow social worker, Addams (right) proclaims the cause to which she devoted much of her life. She won the Nobel Peace Prize in 1931.

NINE

"A Wonderful Time in Which to Live"

On December 10, 1931, a hushed audience in Oslo, Norway, leaned forward to hear the words of a speaker. "She is the foremost woman of her nation," he said. "When the need was greatest she made the American woman's desire for peace an international interest.... She clung to her idealism in the difficult period when other demands and interests overshadowed peace...."

"She" was Jane Addams; the occasion was the awarding of the Nobel Peace Prize. Now 71 years old, she had at last received official recognition for her tireless efforts on behalf of peace. (Established by Swedish millionaire Alfred Nobel, the prize was first awarded in 1901. Addams was the second woman to receive it; the first was Austrian writer and peace worker Bertha von Suttner, in 1905.) Addams did not accept the honor in person; on December 10, she was awaiting lung surgery at Johns Hopkins Hospital in Baltimore, Maryland.

As soon as the prize was announced, the hospital was flooded with cables and letters from all over the world. Among the first to congratulate Addams were President Herbert Hoover, her old colleague at the Food Administration, and John J. "Black Jack" Pershing, the general who had led America's armies into France during World War I. Addams's receipt of the prize marked a full circle in the public's attitude toward her. Once a "saint," then a "villain," she had now regained her position as America's "First Woman."

Most publications, even newspapers that had accused her of anti-Americanism and treason, reported

Alfred Nobel's invention of dynamite made him a millionaire. Perhaps hoping to offset his contribution to war, he endowed an annual award for peace.

the Nobel award as a triumph. The *New York Times*, which called her a "bold crusader for peace," labeled her work "an ultimate expression of an essentially American democracy of spirit," noting that she had always felt an "intense sense of kinship with every member of the human race."

Others praised her for sticking to her principles. "When we entered the war," said one writer, "Miss Addams fought with unexampled courage for free speech, and although she was pilloried in the ribald press, she never flinched from the clamor. She has

never changed her opinions or apologized for them, and for that reason America is proud of the honor conferred upon her."

The day after the Nobel award ceremony, Addams's doctors removed a tumor in her lung. Her health had been deteriorating in the past several years; afflicted with chronic bronchitis, she had also suffered a minor heart attack and, despite medical advice, had gained excessive weight. At 200 pounds, she no longer possessed inexhaustible energy. Nevertheless, she did not even consider retiring from her many activities. "I have been asked," she said, "if I have the courage to begin my work over again. I can only say that it takes more courage to abandon one's principles and habits of life than to keep on with them."

The Nobel Prize carried a cash award of $16,000, an enormous sum in 1931. Addams added it to the $10,000 in prize money she had received from various sources and quietly divided it up between the Women's International League for Peace and Hull House. She was particularly concerned about increasing unemployment among her Chicago neighbors. The Great Depression, triggered by the collapse of the stock market in 1929, was taking a serious toll on America's workers; by 1932, more than 12 million people, 25 percent of the nation's work force, were unemployed.

"I have watched fear grip the people

Presidential candidate Franklin D. Roosevelt (right) and running mate John N. Garner greet voters before the 1932 election that swept them into office.

Secretary of Labor Frances Perkins (left), America's first woman cabinet member, receives an award from First Lady Eleanor Roosevelt in 1934.

in our neighborhood around Hull House," Addams wrote, "men and women who have seen the small margin of their savings disappear; heads of families who see and anticipate hunger for their children before it occurs. That clutch of cold fear is one of the most hideous aspects, I think, of human nature."

In 1932, Herbert Hoover ran for a second term as president against Democrat Franklin D. Roosevelt, who pledged to bring the country out of the Depression. Addams loyally backed her old friend Hoover, but when Roosevelt won in a landslide, she quickly

joined forces with his New Deal administration. Her first move was to work toward the appointment of Frances Perkins, a former Hull House volunteer, as secretary of labor. The effort was successful; Perkins became the first woman cabinet member in American history.

Addams strongly endorsed most of Roosevelt's actions. Among them was the establishment of the Public Works Administration (PWA), a massive federal agency that put the unemployed to work building public housing and other needed projects. Addams served on the Chicago advisory committee for

Relief workers distribute bread to unemployed men and women in 1930. Like most Americans, Addams's Chicago neighbors were hard-hit by the Great Depression.

Preparing to attend the 20th-anniversary celebration of the Women's International League in May 1935, Addams chats with reporters in Washington, D.C.

the PWA, which eventually undertook three major slum-clearance projects near Hull House.

She was naturally delighted by the construction of new housing for her neighbors. In an exuberant 1934 letter to a friend, she wrote about the success of the New Deal in improving the lives of the poor. "It really is a wonderful time in which to live," she said.

Addams's unfailing optimism, combined with her genuine love for other people, continued to win her new friends as she grew older. In his biography, James Linn recalled a young reporter's comments about her. "It isn't so much that you hear she is somebody," said the newsman, "as that she is such a damned nice old lady you can't help falling for her."

Another view came from a volunteer who was describing Addams's return to Hull House after a long trip. "The first thing I heard," recalled the young woman, "was her voice. I heard it all the way from the third floor the minute she walked into the house. There isn't any other voice like it. . . . When I walked downstairs and saw her sitting there in a black velvet dress and her heavy amber beads . . . I felt as if she had been sitting there always, as if there must have been something unfinished about the room all the time she wasn't there."

Although Addams traveled less as she grew older, she kept in constant contact with the many organizations of which she was a member. First in her heart, after Hull House, was the Women's International League. In the spring of 1935, she went to Washington, D.C., to attend a celebration of the peace organization's 20th anniversary. When she got there, she discovered that the occasion was a tribute to her, featuring toasts and speeches from a galaxy of social workers, politicians, writers, and other public figures.

Among the guests was Eleanor Roosevelt, wife of the president. Roosevelt, whom Addams much admired, made a speech in which she called the social worker "a pioneer who is still pioneering." Interior Secretary Harold Ickes, the evening's final speaker, said, "Jane Addams has dared to believe that the Declaration of Independence and the Constitution of the United States were written in good faith and that the rights declared in them are rights that are available to the humblest of our citizens. She is the truest American I have ever known, and there has been none braver."

Addams's response to the shower of praise was characteristic: "I do not know any such person as you have described here tonight," she said. "I have never been sure that I was right; I think we all have to feel our way, step by step." She then made a short but heartfelt speech to her fellow peace workers: "We may be a long way from permanent peace, and we may have a long journey ahead of us in educating

Mourners crowd the Hull House courtyard during Addams's funeral. Afterward, a policeman stopped traffic until her hearse passed. "She goes in peace," he said.

the community and public opinion. Ours may not be an inspiring role. But it tests our endurance and our moral enterprise, and we must see that we keep on."

Addams's health, however, would no longer allow her to "keep on." She returned to Chicago after the Washington tribute; there, two weeks later, she was reading a book when she was suddenly stricken with abdominal pains. Alarmed friends called for an ambulance. "Perhaps," said Addams, "the patient should say a few last words. How long before the ambulance is supposed to be here?" When she

was told it would be 15 minutes, she smiled. "Then I can finish this novel," she said. "There are only a few pages left, and I'd like to get through them."

After surgery, which revealed an advanced case of cancer, Addams rallied briefly. "The hardest thing in the world," she said, "is to kill an old woman." Two days later, however, she lapsed into a coma. Within hours, Jane Addams was dead at the age of 74. It was May 21, 1935.

At Hull House, where Addams's body lay in state, a stream of neighbors, friends, and admirers filed past her casket at the rate of 2,000 per hour. A huge crowd packed the courtyard for the funeral; outside, thousands of silent people lined the rooftops, fire escapes, and streets. Shops, restaurants, even saloons, closed their doors. After the service, the casket was taken by train to Cedarville; there Jane Addams was buried near her beloved father. The stone marking her grave carried only the simple words she had requested: "Jane Addams of Hull House and The Women's International League for Peace."

Her death unleashed a wave of national mourning and a torrent of extravagant praise. Newspapers, magazines, and public speakers compared her to Abraham Lincoln, to St. Francis of Assisi, to Justice Oliver Wendell Holmes, even to the Virgin Mary. She was called "the greatest woman in the United States," "the greatest woman in the world," "the greatest woman in history." Some writers, however, took a more balanced approach, which would probably have pleased Addams more.

"Much nonsense has been written about Miss Addams as 'the angel of Hull House,'" said the *Christian Century*. "The mistaken purpose has been to establish a traditional figure of the St. Francis sort—the figure of a woman who [wanted] to share her crusts as she passed from tenement door to tenement door."

But Addams, asserted the magazine, "had no interest in descending to the poverty level. Her interest was in lifting the level of all about her to new heights. For that reason . . . the emphasis [at Hull House] was on the maximum of enjoyment to be extracted from the widest possible spread of human interests and activities."

Addams was neither saint nor villain. She was a hardheaded idealist, a woman of strong convictions for which she worked hard, and to which she remained faithful. She loved beauty, but she looked straight at the ugliness of Chicago's slums and then made them her home. She loved peace, but she fought countless battles for other people and for her right to speak her mind. A gentle person, she unflinchingly faced criticism and even outright hatred.

One of Jane Addams's legacies is Hull House itself, still operating in Chicago. Another is the continuing vigor of the settlement-house movement she helped establish. In the United States today, more than 600 neighborhoods are served by such centers. Still another legacy is the set of laws that protect today's children; some of the first regulations prohibiting child labor resulted from Addams's work.

But perhaps her principal legacy is the lesson of her life: She demonstrated that one woman could make a difference, not only in her own community and during her own lifetime but in many cities and for many years into the future.

FURTHER READING

Abbot, Edith. *Some American Pioneers in American Social Welfare.* Chicago: University of Chicago Press, 1938.

Addams, Jane. *The Second Twenty Years at Hull House.* New York: Macmillan, 1930.

————. *Twenty Years at Hull House.* New York: New American Library, 1981.

Bennett, Helen Christine. *American Women in Civic Work.* New York: Dodd, Mead, 1915.

Davis, Allen F. *American Heroine: The Life and Legend of Jane Addams.* New York: Oxford University Press, 1973.

Farrell, John C. *Beloved Lady: A History of Jane Addams' Ideas on Reform and Peace.* Baltimore: Johns Hopkins Press, 1967.

Johnson, Emily Cooper, Ed. *Jane Addams: A Centennial Reader.* New York: Macmillan, 1960.

Lasch, Christopher. *The Social Thought of Jane Addams.* Indianapolis: Bobbs-Merrill, 1965.

Levine, Daniel. *Jane Addams and the Liberal Tradition.* Westport, CT: Greenwood, 1980.

Linn, James Weber. *Jane Addams, A Biography.* Westport, CT: Greenwood, 1968.

Unger, Leonard, E. *American Writers.* New York: Scribner, 1979.

CHRONOLOGY

Sept. 6, 1860	Jane Addams born in Cedarville, Illinois
1881	Graduates from Rockford Seminary in Rockford, Illinois
1888	Visits Toynbee Hall, a settlement house in London, England
1889	Opens Hull House, a Chicago community center for the poor
1891	Organizes the Jane Club, a cooperative residence for working women
1892	Establishes Chicago's first public playground
	Publishes a Hull House report about child-labor abuse, resulting in the passage of reform laws
1896	Visits Russian novelist and philosopher Leo Tolstoy in Moscow
1902	Publishes *Democracy and Social Ethics*
1907	Publishes *Newer Ideals of Peace*
1909	Becomes founding member of the National Association for the Advancement of Colored People
	Publishes *The Spirit of Youth and the City Streets*
1910	Publishes autobiography, *Twenty Years at Hull House*
1911	Becomes vice-president of the National American Woman Suffrage Association
1912	Publishes *A New Conscience and an Ancient Evil*
	Campaigns for presidential candidate Theodore Roosevelt
1914	Becomes leader of Emergency Federation of Peace Forces as World War I begins in Europe
1915	Helps form and is elected chairperson of the Woman's Peace Party; stirs public outrage with antiwar speech
1918	Joins Herbert Hoover's Food Administration after the United States enters the war
1919	Elected president of the Women's International League for Peace and Freedom
1920	Incites public wrath by defending alleged communists and anarchists
1922	Publishes *Peace and Bread in Time of War*
1931	Receives Nobel Peace Prize
1932	Serves with Public Works Administration under President Franklin D. Roosevelt
May 21, 1935	Dies of cancer

INDEX

INDEX

PICTURE CREDITS

Mary Kittredge is a novelist and biographer whose other Chelsea House books for young adults include *Marc Antony* and *Frederick the Great.*

Matina S. Horner is president of Radcliffe College and associate professor of psychology and social relations at Harvard University. She is best known for her studies of women's motivation, achievement, and personality development. Dr. Horner serves on several national boards and advisory councils, including those of the National Science Foundation, Time Inc., and the Women's Research and Education Institute. She earned her B.A. from Bryn Mawr College and Ph.D. from the University of Michigan, and holds honorary degrees from many colleges and universities, including Mount Holyoke, Smith, Tufts, and the University of Pennsylvania.